Business School

GW00493108

Book 5

Different ways of looking at business

Coordinated and written by Kirstie Ball with contributions from Diane Preston, George Watson, Fran Myers, Anja Schaefer and Penny Marrington

The Open University Walton Hall, Milton Keynes MK7 6AA

First published 2006. Second edition 2010. Third edition 2011.

© 2011 The Open University

All rights reserved. No part of this publication may be reproduced, stored in a retrieval system, transmitted or utilised in any form or by any means, electronic, mechanical, photocopying, recording or otherwise, without written permission from the publisher or a licence from the Copyright Licensing Agency Ltd. Details of such licences (for reprographic reproduction) may be obtained from the Copyright Licensing Agency Ltd, Saffron House, 6–10 Kirby Street, London EC1N 8TS (website: www.cla.co.uk).

Open University course materials may also be made available in electronic formats for use by students of the University. All rights, including copyright and related rights and database rights, in electronic course materials and their contents are owned by or licensed to The Open University, or otherwise used by The Open University as permitted by applicable law.

In using electronic course materials and their contents you agree that your use will be solely for the purposes of following an Open University course of study or otherwise as licensed by The Open University or its assigns.

Except as permitted above you undertake not to copy, store in any medium (including electronic storage or use in a website), distribute, transmit or retransmit, broadcast, modify or show in public such electronic materials in whole or in part without the prior written consent of The Open University or in accordance with the Copyright, Designs and Patents Act 1988.

Edited and designed by The Open University.

Printed and bound in the United Kingdom by Charlesworth Press, Wakefield.

ISBN 978 1 8487 3589 7

3.1

Contents

Introduction   5
    Aims and objectives   6
    Structure   7

Session 1 Looking at business more critically   8
    1.1 Challenging traditional views   8
    1.2 Different ways of seeing business   11
    1.3 What does all this mean for students of business?   15
    1.4 'Check your understanding' quiz   20
    1.5 Conclusion   22
    1.6 Learning outcomes   22

Session 2 The history of business thinking   23
    2.1 Different views   23
    2.2 The context of B120 in the current business environment   24
    2.3 History of business thinking and writing   25
    2.4 The future: globalisation and corporate power   29
    2.5 Conclusion   31
    2.6 Learning outcomes   31

Session 3 Globalisation   32
    3.1 What is globalisation?   32
    3.2 Internationalisation and globalisation   33
    3.3 Drivers of globalisation   34
    3.4 Multinational corporations   38
    3.5 Conclusion   40
    3.6 Learning outcomes   40

Session 4 Business and power   41
    4.1 Power and influence   41
    4.2 The dimensions of power   42
    4.3 Conclusion   50
    4.4 Learning outcomes   50

Session 5 Resisting and challenging business power   51
    5.1 Negative business power   51
    5.2 Controlling business power   52
    5.3 Conclusion   61
    5.4 Learning outcomes   61

Summary of Book 5   62

References   64

Acknowledgements   65

Module team   65

Introduction

Welcome to Book 5 of B120. In an introduction to business studies course such as B120 it is important that we provide you with a comprehensive understanding of the main topics of concern in the business literature. It is also important that you are aware of some of the 'classical' models such as ***Taylor's scientific management***, ***Hofstede's cultural difference model***, ***Morgan's 'metaphor' model***, ***Porter's 'five forces model'***, ***Maslow's hierarchy of needs*** and ***Vroom's expectancy theory***, to name but a few. You were introduced to these models in earlier B120 course books and we mention them again briefly in the context of this book. (If you are worried that you can't remember what they are, you will find them in the Glossary!)

Up to now in the course we have talked about businesses as having certain consistent features. You will remember, for example, that in Book 1 we talked about the similarities we might look for across businesses: a structure of some kind, a culture, an external environment, an ethical code or a set of values. We also started to explore what was different about businesses; for example, technology, location, size and life cycle. This final book of the course introduces another key learning point about business. This is that a particular point of view, or ***paradigm***, tends to dominate much of the literature about business and the way it is taught. This is often called the ***rationalist*** perspective (that is, based on reason and logic), which we shall also refer to as the ***traditional*** way of looking at a business. It is important to realise, however, that other frames of analysis exist as well. In business, as in life, there are always different ways of seeing the same things; it just depends on where you are looking from.

To highlight this idea of differing perceptions, look at the picture below. Do you see an old woman or a young woman, or both? Does the picture vary each time you look?

This is a commonly used demonstration of perception. If you have difficulty seeing both, concentrate on the nose/chin of the woman you do see.

You may remember Morgan's (1986) model (Book 1, Session 1, section 1.3) of the different metaphors we could use to think about businesses in different ways. You can refresh your memory of Morgan's model now (or later) if you have Book 1 available. In reminding you of the model, our intention is not so much to rehearse the eight metaphors Morgan suggests (which are a machine, an organism, a brain, a culture, a political system, a psychic prison, flux and transformation and a vehicle for domination), but to prepare you for this book in which we will begin to think about businesses from alternative perspectives. As always, we recommend the concurrent use of your B120 Study Companion to help you get the most out of your learning from this book.

In business, again as in life, our perceptions govern our interpretations of the world around us. After studying this book, you will realise that there are multiple perceptions and interpretations of business activities. These views are held not just by individuals, but also collectively in groups or wider society. And it is these, 'alternative', views of business that will be the overarching theme in this final book of the course. You might say that, having set up all these relatively neat models of business in Books 1 to 4, we are now going to take them apart – this is the fun of learning! By this stage in the course you will probably feel more confident about starting to challenge some of the assumptions that can be found in the business literature. Not taking things at face value is an extremely important study skill that you will have been developing throughout the course.

Aims and objectives

The aims of Book 5 are to:

- identify a dominant paradigm in the business literature about what a business is and how it operates;
- explain the critical view of business which offers an alternative perspective and challenges many of the taken-for-granted assumptions about managing and controlling business activities;
- describe some basic philosophical ideas about how we view the world;
- discuss how business and management thinking has developed over time;
- appreciate the cultural and international context in which modern businesses operate;
- explain the relationship between business and power at the levels of individual, group, business and society;
- challenge your thinking and develop your study skills in preparation for further study with The Open University.

Structure

Book 5 is divided into five study sessions:

Session 1	challenges traditional views of business and introduces some alternative perspectives on business knowledge.
Session 2	examines the history of business thinking and its influences, and takes a look at the future of business.
Session 3	explores the globalisation debate and the challenges facing multinational corporations.
Session 4	takes you into the complex and controversial world of business and its economic and social power.
Session 5	examines what happens when corporations go too far, and how their actions can be resisted and challenged.

Session 1 Looking at business more critically

Why are we studying 'looking at business more critically'? Traditional business literature tends to adopt a rather unproblematic view of how businesses operate. As students of business studies, we need to be aware that there are other, more critical perspectives on the business world.

The **aims and objectives** of Session 1 are to:

- define the philosophical concepts of reification, **_ontology_** and **_epistemology_** (these and other terms you will come across in this book are defined in the Glossary);

- explain the difference between traditional and critical views of business;

- explain that only partial control can be achieved by the managers of a business;

- explain the difference between positivist and interpretivist or phenomenological approaches within social science (which includes business studies);

- explore the problems specific to generating knowledge about business;

- explore these ideas in the analysis of a case study.

1.1 Challenging traditional views

The majority of textbooks about business tend to talk about businesses as things or objects. In other words, they treat them as a '**_black box_**' whose existence and nature is taken for granted and is unquestionable. A more critical stance would emphasise that business is more about the sets of understandings and behaviours of the people who work _in_ a business, and the economic, social and political systems and **_institutions_** that surround it. In philosophy, viewing phenomena as unquestionable objects or things is a process called 'reification'.

When a concept becomes 'reified', it is treated, in arguments and conversation, as if it actually exists, is tangible and can be grasped, owned and used by people, organisations and society. This is often in spite of the fact that it is only ever an abstract concept. Reification in itself is not a particularly controversial idea; in fact, it can help us establish a dramatic impact for what we say. However, it is unwise, in the context of learning, knowledge and education to reify abstract concepts because it leads us to form inaccurate, incorrect or fallacious arguments. For example, take the tag line of the well-known television programme _The X Files_: 'The truth is out there'. This statement reifies 'truth' as a physical object which is 'discoverable' and is somewhere specific, whereas truth is an abstract property of knowledge claims and is not located anywhere. It would be more correct to say 'The truth about a certain issue is something we can discover if we try hard enough'.

One of the key purposes of Book 5 is to encourage you to start to think more critically about business and how we tend to write about it. For example, the usual assumption underlying business studies is that it is possible to achieve a high level of rational control over work behaviour. This is for very pragmatic economic reasons: businesses operate in a world of scarce resources. They need to monitor and control their utilisation of such resources in order to ensure the most efficient outputs. However, ethical, political and social questions arise when such approaches are applied to the people who work in businesses.

A related question is whether there is a single key to business success. Constant change in the business world means that there is rarely one solution to a problem, and the solutions take no heed of the constant change. The last time you looked at a bookshop in an airport, for example, or at the business section of your local bookshop, you would have seen bestselling titles such as *In Search of Excellence* by T. J. Peters and R. H. Waterman and *The One Minute Manager* by K. H. Blanchard and S. Johnson. If you were to do a Web search for books on leadership, you would wonder at the inventiveness that goes into thinking of titles for books about how to be successful in business.

You may be surprised to learn that theories about business and management are a relatively recent phenomenon. The academic subject of business studies came about largely as a result of people wanting to develop careers in business and management, and the growth of institutions teaching business has been immense. The study of business is usually divided into different areas such as operations management, strategic management, consumer behaviour, and so on. This division of study into separate subjects is rather like the predominant approach that these studies themselves adopt: we make it manageable by treating business as a static entity that can be carved up in this way. As with business itself, this is rather far from reality; internal and external influences and business functions actually work together in a complex and integrated way.

Watson (2002) provides an alternative view of business (and society):

> To treat either 'society' or 'the organisation' as something that can itself take initiatives, make choices or impose its 'will' on human beings is to leave out of the analysis the fact that the social and organisational world is made – and is constantly being 'remade' – by human actions. And these are not politically neutral human actions: power, persuasion, resistance, knowledge, ignorance and ambiguity play a major part in every aspect of societal and organisational activity.
>
> (Watson, 2002, p. 49)

This view is sometimes called the 'critical' perspective. The intention is to encourage us to stop and think more about what is going on beneath the surface of everyday business life. A critical approach would ask questions such as the following. How realistic is it to think that we can control people and their work? Can individuals really be managed in this way and is it morally acceptable to try? A critical 'take' on human resource management, for example, might be that it is a business function concerned with 'rendering the individual knowable in order to facilitate management control' (Townley, 1994, p. 12). In other words, isn't managing people about getting them to do what you want them to do?

We might argue that businesses are not 'real' in the sense that they do not comprise a physical entity as such, but we still have to find a way of relating to them. They are capable, after all, of employing us, taxing us, entertaining us, feeding us; in short, they can have an immense impact on our lives. But when you think about it, businesses are as much about how the systems, inputs, outputs, relationships, and so on, are understood by people as about those systems themselves. We might say, then, that businesses have a virtual reality. This is a difficult but important idea in business studies and, as we have already suggested, actually takes us into the realms of philosophy. If you are interested in finding out more about the intangible aspects of business, particularly in marketing and branding, you might like to look at Additional Readings 5.1 and 5.2 in the B120 online resources.

We now need to introduce another new word, 'ontology', which refers to how sure we can be that something actually exists. In other words, ontology is the study of being and existence. However, as this is not a philosophy course, we will not go into any further detail here. The key point for your study of B120 is that, however uncomfortable it might make us feel (or however annoying we find the discussion of what is real and what is not), as a student of business it is important that we learn to ask such questions as:

- What is a business really like?
- What is it really like to work there?
- How can we really know anything about the way in which businesses are organised?

'Keep in mind, this is just a daydream I'm having while I'm lying on the beach.'

When we read or hear about business in the media, in journal articles and in textbooks, it is important to question how the accounts or stories we are reading have been put together. Did the author talk to everyone in the business and make a reasoned judgement? Did they talk to just a few people? Did they consult any statistics? If so, whose statistics were they and how were they generated? On what basis have the things that we read been compiled and should we believe them to be 'true' or 'representative' of the phenomena they are describing?

Bearing in mind this idea of a somehow 'virtual' business, give some thought to the poor managers whose job it is to control businesses. Remember that 'traditional' business literature deals with the problem of management by, first, accepting unquestionably the divide between those individuals who manage and those who are managed and, second, treating the business as a thing that can be designed, measured and controlled.

Treating businesses and other phenomena associated with them as if they are real, tangible and 'out there' makes it easier to think about them and quantify what happens. We should, however, be careful to avoid any inaccuracies arising from this 'reification' of business. The critical perspective reminds us of this, and is based on two important limitations:

1   Only partial control can ever be achieved. This is because businesses exist only through human relationships, and human relationships never allow the total control of some people over others; hence the difficulties inherent in 'managing people'.

2   Whatever control is actually achieved over collective and individual business behaviour is brought about as much by processes of persuasion, manipulation, negotiation and sometimes basic chemistry between people as through 'techniques' such as rules and procedures (Watson, 2002, p. 61).

One of the biggest challenges we face when thinking and talking about businesses and how to manage them is that we could suggest that they do not actually *exist*, or that they certainly don't exist in the way that, say, this book you are reading exists. You cannot actually touch a business or pick it up, throw it across the room or put it away for later. Businesses are not static, concrete entities that stay the same over time.

1.2 Different ways of seeing business

Up to this point, our intention has been threefold:

1   to establish that there are many different ways of seeing the world and things in it, including businesses;

2   to recognise that there tends to be a predominant way of analysing businesses within the business literature;

3   to acknowledge that all perspectives are both helpful and limiting to us in some way.

How, then, do we now go about making judgements about the relative value of one point of view and/or piece of analysis or knowledge compared with another? This takes us into another area of philosophy: issues of epistemology. Epistemology is the branch of philosophy that deals with the nature, origin and scope of knowledge. You need to refer to your Glossary to make sure you understand terms like this.

When it comes to understanding human behaviour, there are two contrasting 'epistemologies' which we can use. The first is called the ***positivist*** view which claims that, as part of the natural world, human behaviour should be examined using methods comparable to those used to study the natural world. In other words, we can somehow measure human behaviour using scientific methods, and design experiments which work out whether behaviours are predictable in certain circumstances, and so on. The second epistemology is called the ***interpretivist*** (also referred to as the ***phenomenological***) view of behaviour, which claims that, because humans are self-interpreting (we attach meanings to what we do), they cannot be studied in the same way as other natural phenomena. These two competing points of view actually form the two ends of a continuum: there are a number of 'positions' in between that are beyond the scope of our discussion here. It is important, however, that you understand the basic differences between these two main approaches.

In social science subjects such as business studies there is frequently no 'right answer'. Everything depends on the perspective you adopt, and whether that particular perspective is appropriate for the problem you are intending to solve, or the issue you want to investigate. For example, if we were to adopt a more 'positivist' approach to business, we would want to invent ways to measure different phenomena; we would attempt to make so many observations that we could estimate or predict what was going to happen; we would try to generate rules and laws about what is likely to happen under particular sets of circumstances; and we would try to control or manipulate situations by changing the inputs according to our predictions. Frequently, in business the picture is more fuzzy. We cannot always see business phenomena because they are not tangible (for example, how do you identify and measure 'culture'?). People change over time, so a view they present as a certainty one year, may have changed two or three years later in the light of their experience. Overall, whether we can say, with any level of certainty, that something is 'true' largely depends on our starting point, the resources we use to analyse the problem at hand and the language and conventions we use to aid our descriptions. Essentially, our understandings of, and assertions about, businesses are not 'true' in any finite sense, they are simply 'truth claims' that will hold for a particular period of time, within a particular context of application (for example, within one industry or sector, one particular type of business, or in respect of one particular group of employees).

Specific problems are also associated with the nature of businesses, and we need to keep an open mind about how we view these. These are described by Bryman (1989) as:

1   levels of analysis

2   measuring organisational effectiveness

3   problems of time

4   the problem of paradigms.

These four problems are now discussed in more detail.

Levels of analysis

By now you will be familiar with the idea that businesses are made up of different types of structural hierarchies. (Business structures were discussed in Book 1, study Session 3). When we look at a business, either one for which we work or one we read about (for example, in a case study), one of the first things we recognise is how the business is structured. This is about who can tell whom what to do, who occupies which role, and what the nature of each role is. However, when we are solving business problems, we need to think about who or what in particular we are analysing and to whom or to what our solution applies at a more general level. Typically, a business comprises individual members of staff, groups of staff, departments and their subunits, and the whole business operates within a specific environment. So, we need to adopt an approach that is suitable for the problem we are solving. At the level of the individual, problems (for example, persistent lateness or absenteeism) require a solution tailored to those individuals who are persistently late or absent. At the level of the group, problems, such as securing effective team performance, will require an approach which looks at the way the whole team works: any solutions we come up with can then be applied to other teams. Similarly, it would be pointless trying to analyse the market behaviour of a whole business by using individual psychology, and it would be difficult to understand how a whole department worked by using theories about small groups. Hence, when we analyse a business we need to identify the level at which we are analysing it. In other words, is what we are saying applicable only to individuals in the business? Or is it applicable to groups, departments or the whole business?

The diagram in Figure 1.1 will help you to think about *levels of analysis*. Imagine that the different levels are all 'embedded' within one another. Individuals are *embedded* within groups or teams, which form departments, which together form the organisation, which in turn operates in an environment containing other organisations.

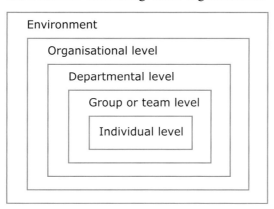

Figure 1.1 Levels of analysis

Measuring organisational effectiveness

The second issue identified by Bryman is the problem of effectiveness. When we analyse a business case, we tend to focus on solving problems and recommending solutions. Invariably, the viability of each solution we propose is dependent on whether it will actually make things more efficient and improve business performance. However, from an academic point of view, each business has its own *performance indicators*: measures and scores by which it knows it is achieving its objectives. And, when it comes to comparing businesses, there is no coherent theory or standard measure of what effectiveness is. One way round this is to ask, before comparing a business with others, whether that business is achieving the goals it has set itself, and whether it is using its resources in the way that it intended.

Problems of time

We have mentioned how people's perceptions can change in the light of experience, and the same is true for businesses. Constant shifting of managerial interpretations and belief systems can make a highly prioritised set of actions obsolete within months. For the business analyst, time also presents a problem because the start and finish of events in business is often unclear. For example, how could you define the beginning and end of the installation of a new computer system? Does it begin when an IT manager writes a tender document to prospective suppliers? Or when the supplier turns up at the business ready to change everything over? Does the process end when the supplier leaves the building, or when each user is fully trained on the system and has modified their working patterns where necessary? What would be your reasons for defining it in a particular way?

The problem of paradigms

Earlier in this study session we introduced the idea that there are two contrasting ways of studying human behaviour (the positivist and interpretivist or phenomenological) which can be applied to businesses. Because the assumptions of each are incompatible, it is necessary to choose one over the other. However, in doing so, we are trading off valuable information. Moreover, within the field of business theory, '*paradigm wars*' have emerged, where various eminent professors spend much time at academic conferences arguing about which is the more effective and fruitful in terms of research findings. Others argue that it is possible to combine perspectives, but only within very tightly defined ***parameters***. Ultimately, whether you think a positivist or interpretivist stance is preferable will depend not only on the kind of problem you are trying to solve, but also on your personal views as to which is the most beneficial, and why.

Activity 1.1

Spend about **30 minutes** on this activity

Purpose: to clarify the difference between the positivist and the interpretivist or phenomenological approach.

Task: as a manager within a large supermarket business, you are asked to carry out a ***time and motion study*** of the work of the employees on the checkout. A time and motion study is a systematic logging of the time it takes each person to complete a task (in this case putting a complete order through the checkout) and then analysing the individual and collective results to produce an 'ideal' time for the task. When you publish the results of your study, the checkout team argue that it isn't fair to apply this measure to Saturday working as several parttime students are employed on Saturdays, who, they claim, work at a much slower rate. How would you approach this issue, first using a positivist approach, and then using an interpretivist or phenomenological approach? What are the relative advantages and disadvantages of each?

Feedback

A time and motion study is itself a positivist approach to the understanding of work. The fact that some of the staff objected to its use, on the grounds that it overlooked the needs of a particular group of employees, highlights shortfalls in positivist approaches, which can be addressed by using a phenomenological approach to the problem at hand. Despite being an efficient and 'scientific' approach, specific problems associated with the positivist approach include:

- a general, 'one size fits all' approach;
- the assumption that everyone is the same, and produces the same outputs in the same circumstances;
- the assumption that people work in the same way as machines.

An interpretivist approach would involve spending time with all the different groups of workers. You could review their performance and their pay, and establish different work rates for different times of day. The advantage of this is that the workers would be more likely to accept changes in work rates because they had been consulted. You could also use this data to inform a more detailed and varied time and motion study. The disadvantage is that this approach is very labour intensive and cannot be conducted on a very large scale.

1.3 What does all this mean for students of business?

Ultimately, when we come to study and analyse businesses we must reflect on and be absolutely clear about the boundaries and parameters of our analysis: what we can and cannot do with the information we have in front of us, and what we can and cannot say with the analytical resources and theories we are using. This is a process called *critical reflection*, and is a key skill to develop and use throughout all your future studies.

When reflecting critically on a business problem we would typically consider:

- whether a viable solution can be achieved by measuring different aspects of the situation to predict the likely outcome, or by talking to different people within the business to establish their views and preferences;
- at what level of analysis the problem lies and whether the solutions we propose and the theories we use are applicable at that level;
- whether there are any proposed benefits of the solution and how they would be assessed;
- the nature of the time parameters surrounding the problem;

- whether different groups are likely to comply with the solution we propose. At a more general level this means considering the implications for power balances, control relationships and resistance in the business.

We are now going to explore the ideas we have just discussed through the following case study. Before reading the case study, take a look at the task for Activity 1.2 which follows it.

Case Study 1.1

Handy Snack (Distributing) Company

Handy Snack (Distributing) Co is a food and drink distribution company with more than 1500 employees and gross annual sales in excess of £52 million. The company purchases snack foods (peanuts, crisps, etc.) as well as bottled and tinned drinks (ranging from fruit juices to exotic alcoholic cocktail drinks), and distributes them to independent retailers throughout the UK and Ireland. Competition in the industry is intense and competitors are continually updating product lines in a bid to gain market share.

Handy Snack has nine regional centres (seven in the UK and two in Ireland), each with its own warehouse, sales staff, and finance and purchasing departments. Since the company's inception 12 years ago, the head office in London has always encouraged each region to be autonomous because of well-recognised variations in localised product demand. For example, the demand for cocktail drinks and the more exotic snacks is highest in the South-east region of the UK, while in the South-west consumers prefer cider and lager beers, and more traditional snacks.

5 years ago, the Board of Directors expressed a desire to have more detailed information on the performance of each region. Consequently, head office introduced a centralised financial reporting system which enabled the Board to compare sales, costs and profits across the nine regions. Each region was treated as a profit centre and the system revealed that profit margins varied markedly from region to region. As these differences became more pronounced, Michael Rosen, the company chairman, decided that a degree of standardisation needed to be imposed. He suspected that some regions were sometimes using lower-quality products in a bid to increase regional profitability and was eager to put a stop to such practices before any harm could be done to the company's reputation for high-quality products. Certainly it was true that most regions were facing cut-throat competition from the larger distributing and discounting organisations who were cutting prices and launching innovative new products in a bid to increase market share.

In order to achieve the required degree of standardisation, Michael Rosen decided to create a new managerial post to oversee the company's regional pricing and purchasing policies. The post was filled by Peter Borden, who was previously employed as a senior finance manager by Handy Snack's closest business rival, National Distributing.

Borden reported directly to Pauline Pedder, managing director of finance.

In line with the non-bureaucratic ethos of the company, Pedder encouraged Borden to develop whatever procedures he thought necessary to achieve the desired outcome. Each regional director was notified of Borden's appointment by an official memorandum and it was also announced in the company bi-monthly newsletter.

As he analysed the accounts, Borden decided that two problems needed tackling. Over the long term, Handy Snack should make better use of information technology. He believed information technology could provide timely and accurate information to enable head office to make higher-quality decisions. At present, top managers in the regions were connected to head office by an electronic mail system, but no other employees or sales people were connected.

In truth, head office had experienced considerable difficulty in getting any senior managers to use the E-mail system on a regular basis. The head office in London had even started to receive anonymous messages (presumably from the regional offices). Although harmless enough (e.g. 'Big Brother is Watching You!' and 'Contrary to popular belief, London is not the centre of the Universe!') these messages were perhaps symptomatic of the resentment felt by some regions – particularly those in Scotland and Ireland – at what they saw as head office interference in regional affairs.

For his part, Borden put the spate of anonymous messages down to seasonal high spirits (Christmas was only 8 weeks away) and the problems created by a lack of corporate centralisation. Certainly his experience at National Distributing (a highly centralised organisation) had led him to value strong corporate leadership and control.

In the short term, Borden decided that fragmented pricing and purchasing decisions were a problem. To him the solution was obvious – such decisions should be standardised across all the regions. As a first step, he wanted the financial executive in each region to notify him of any changes in local prices. He also decided that all new contracts for local purchasing (approximately 35 per cent of items purchased) should be cleared through his office.

Borden discussed the proposed changes with Pauline Pedder. She agreed and they submitted a formal proposal to Rosen and the board of directors, who approved the plan. These changes represented a significant change in company policy, but Borden was eager to implement the changes as quickly as possible in order to beat the rush of Christmas orders. He decided to send an electronic mail message and a covering fax to all the financial and purchasing executives in each region, notifying them of the new procedures right away.

Borden showed a draft of the message to Pedder and invited her comments. She said that the message was a good idea but wondered if it was appropriate or sufficient. The regions handled hundreds of items and were used to decentralised decision-making.

'It may be helpful if you were to visit our regional offices and discuss these procedural changes with regional management,' Pedder advised. 'The culture here is quite different to National Distributing. We recruit all regional personnel (including senior managers) from the locality – some of them are proud of the fact that they have never visited London head office!'

'I've got far too much to do here without wasting my time travelling, Pauline,' replied Borden.

'Well, why not wait until the annual company meeting?' she suggested. 'Then you could meet all the local managers, and discuss your ideas with them face-to-face.'

'No.' retorted Borden. 'I can't wait that long to bring in these changes. I think it's important that I make my presence felt as soon as possible. I'll send the messages out tomorrow.'

During the next few days, he received electronic mail replies from three of the regions (from managers who said they would be happy to co-operate).

Yet four weeks later, Borden had not received notices from any region about local price or purchase changes. Informal enquiries by Pauline Pedder revealed that the regions were busy as usual following conventional procedures.

Borden decided to telephone one of the regional managers. Much to his chagrin he discovered that she did not know who he was or what his new purchasing procedures were. 'Besides,' she argued, 'we have enough to worry about reaching difficult profit goals seemingly chosen at random by you lot at head office, without additional procedures and "red tape". My region has always been profitable – why not pick on other, less profitable, regions. Noone has ever had cause to change my working practices before. To be honest, I see no logical reason to start doing so now.'

As Christmas approached, Peter Borden came under increasing pressure from the Board to bring all the regions into line with company procedures and standards.

(Source: Corbett, 1994, pp. 190–2)

Activity 1.2

Spend about **1 hour** on this activity

Purpose: to reinforce your understanding of different levels of analysis in business studies.

Task: read carefully Case Study 1.1. It is about the troubled implementation of an information technology system which was supposed to change communication patterns in a snacks and drinks manufacturing business. As you read, first of all try to identify all the problems there are within the case described. Then group these into the levels of analysis at which they occur. Once you have decided which levels of analysis are more important, try to think of some solutions to the problems, which would be applicable at those levels, and how you might go about advising the business.

Feedback

Having read through the case study carefully, you should have identified a number of potential problems in this case at three levels of analysis: the business, the group and the individual.

At the level of the business overall, there is a structural problem which involved balancing the tension between centralisation and decentralisation of power. Borden and Rosen were keen to unite the different regions of the business through systems and reporting.

Communication and organisational culture are also an issue. Only formal channels are used to communicate the proposed changes: interpersonal or face-to-face communication is not used to reinforce them. This, accompanied with poor timing, has rendered the implementation of the email system ineffective and few managers use it.

At a group level it is clear that there are perhaps problems in the cohesiveness of the top management team, and little interaction between different regional managers as a group.

At the individual level there are problems in the interpersonal relationships between Pauline Pedder and Peter Borden. Peter's communication skills need to be improved, the scope of his job description perhaps needs redefining and he needs to be more sensitive to the culture of the business he has recently joined.

You may have identified many solutions to the above problems, but a few are suggested below.

At the business level:

- Allow longer timescales for organisational change.
- Use different techniques for change involving the regions, including greater consultation.
- Rethink the induction package for new directors.

At the group level:

- Implement teambuilding exercises at management team level and across the regions.

At the individual level:

- Put together a tailored induction package for Borden, which features leadership, communication and change training.

Working through this business case study should have reinforced your understanding of different levels of analysis. Your work on this will form the basis of an online tutor group forum discussion for Book 5.

This first study session has introduced many new and challenging ideas in the study of business. We want to end it with a short quiz which will help to highlight some of the key learning points.

1.4 'Check your understanding' quiz

Up to now in this study session, you have been introduced to some complex ideas about business. This may have left you feeling a little uncomfortable. At this point it might be best to review some of these ideas and check your understanding before moving on. We have compiled a light-hearted, yet informative, quiz. You will find the answers in section 1.5 at the end of this study session, but have a go at completing the quiz before you check these!

Activity 1.3

Spend about **10 minutes** on this activity.

Purpose: to clarify your understanding of some of the key terms and ideas introduced in study Session 1.

Task: complete the following multiple choice questions.

1   What is the traditional (or rationalist) view of business?

   (a) It assumes that people and processes can be controlled.

   (b) It tries to go beyond the obvious aspects.

   (c) It considers only old businesses, not new ones.

2   What is epistemology concerned with?

   (a) The nature, origin and scope of knowledge

   (b) The nature of personification.

   (c) The nature of existence.

3   Why would we argue (philosophically) that a business is actually 'virtual' and not real?

   (a) Because of the introduction of online shopping.

   (b) Because we can never expect to totally control the actions and understandings of people.

   (c) Because we want to make business studies more difficult.

4   What is ontology?

(a) The study of business.

(b) The study of being and existence.

(c) The study of birds.

5 Why does the rationalist view of business tend to dominate the business literature? (More than one answer may apply.)

(a) It is easier to think about businesses as concrete entities.

(b) It is preferable to think that we might control business rather than it controlling us.

(c) Managers need to feel they are achieving something in life.

6 Are the following statements about the rationalist view of business true or false?

The rationalist perspective on business is:

(a) Just one of many ways of analysing what a business is – true/false?

(b) Neither right nor wrong – true/false?

Feedback

This quiz was intended to make you stop and think. The kinds of words and ideas we have introduced in this first study session may be very different from what you are used to when thinking about business. The aim of Book 5 is to emphasise that there is always more than one way of analysing a business and that different perspectives and levels of analysis exist which are different from those (rationalist) models that tend to dominate the business literature. Beginning to challenge assumptions is one of the key learning and study skills of this course and one which you will need as you continue your study of the business world in subsequent courses.

'In an increasingly complex world, sometimes old questions require new answers.'

1.5 Conclusion

Now that we have set out the terrain for the rest of the book, we hope that you will have grasped some of the complexities of business studies. You should also have realised by now that most of these complexities are not peculiar to business: indeed, they are inherent in all social science subjects. Social science (as opposed to natural science: to remind yourself, see again Activity 1.1) has the tools to examine the imprecise, uncertain and, in some cases, 'virtual' nature of the business world, and in this study session we have outlined just a few of these tools. In particular, we would like you to bear in mind that within social science there are different approaches to knowledge and knowing. We need to be careful not to automatically reify businesses as objects, and must always question why we tend to perceive them as solid, factual and stable. We can use this to establish alternative ontologies of business, and investigate them using appropriate and contrasting methodologies: positivism and phenomenology. It is important also to realise that business changes over time, that it can be understood at different levels, and that there are multiple definitions of what it is to be 'effective' in business. In the next study session we begin to think about how business has developed over time up to the present day.

1.6 Learning outcomes

By the end of this study session on looking at business more critically you should be able to:

- explain the critical perspective on business;
- describe the difference between the natural and social science approaches to studying business;
- outline the positivist and interpretivist or phenomenological perspectives;
- demonstrate an awareness of specific problems associated with analysing businesses;
- explain the importance, for students of business, of understanding organisational culture.

You will have developed your learning by:

- examining a case study in order to reinforce your understanding of different levels of analysis;
- participating in a light-hearted quiz as an alternative method of reviewing your learning.

[The answers to the quiz are: 1(a), 2(a), 3(b), 4(b), 5(a), (b) and (c), 6 (a) = true, 6(b) = true.]

Session 2 The history of business thinking

Why are we studying 'the history of business thinking'? Any idea, theory or model of how business works and what it needs is to some extent a product of its time. Many of the ideas, theories and models developed in the past remain relevant to businesses today, but it is important to know where ideas have come from and the context in which they emerged.

The **aims and objectives** of Session 2 are to:

- explain that the emergence of business knowledge is partly influenced by what is happening in the wider historical context;
- explain the specific influences, from the twentieth century, of context on business knowledge;
- identify some future issues and questions in the realm of business knowledge.

2.1 Different views

In the last study session, our aim was to establish that understanding business is more than just a simple matter of understanding facts and figures about businesses. It is also a matter of understanding the political, social, technical and environmental origins of particular businesses and markets, and questioning the actions of business from a social science perspective which tells us that (among other things) there isn't a right answer. Academics and researchers writing about business are always influenced by the business, social, political and economic (for example) events of their time.

As you have studied this course, you have gained access to the thoughts of many academics and practitioners in the field of business and management. You may or may not have agreed with their opinions on human resource management, marketing or accounting and finance for a variety of different reasons. You will also have noticed that often they do not agree with each other.

Writers also often present alternative ways of dealing with the same problems that are faced by businesses; these problem solving tools evolve, grow and ebb in popularity over time. During your studies and in your employment, when you need to solve a problem you will often be able to choose the model that best suits the requirements of that particular problem, which may differ depending on whether you are writing an assignment, giving advice to a friend who is about to start their own business, or making a presentation to your boss at work.

In this section we aim to give you a very brief introduction to the context of business thinking, how it changes over time and how business writers draw on other fields such as science, sociology, psychology and philosophy to better understand what is going on in the business environment. We will also try to give you an understanding of how political, social and cultural changes influence writers themselves. So, for example, you can see how differently a woman working in an expanding business in Japan today might think about business, in contrast to an American man writing from a university in the 1950s.

2.2 The context of B120 in the current business environment

The Open University Business School is based in the UK, and the vast majority of the staff is European with a European cultural background. This is also the case for the majority of students. It follows therefore that, although B120 draws widely on the works of, say, US scholars, or brings in examples of how markets in Asia operate, the course may have different outlooks on some business related subjects from another course written in China, for example, by Chinese academics for Chinese business students. Western (that is, European and US) business thinking has concentrated historically on a rationalist approach to business. This was explained in the last study session and involves breaking things down into their constituent parts to analyse how they might best be improved or 'solved'. Eastern thinking has traditionally been more *holistic*, and has looked at how a situation might be improved as whole or, indeed, whether it should be improved at all. Principles such as quality management, which look at a whole process of operations (remember section 6.4 on 'Operations' in Book 1, study Session 6) related to a whole business within its environment, originated in Asian business thinking.

The following section looks at how business thinking in the West is evolving in parallel with key developments in the social and political fields. For the purposes of this book, the examples given are mainly from the UK.

2.3 History of business thinking and writing

Probably the oldest reference materials widely used in businesses today are the compilations of the Chinese General, Sun Tzu, written over 2,000 years ago. *Sun Tzu, The Art of War* (Griffith, 1963) is an influential collection used by company strategists worldwide. Sayings such as 'To win without fighting is best' are popular in company presentations and mission statements. However, thinking about business specifically really began only in the early years of the twentieth century. Figure 2.1 shows parallel timelines of major political events and movements, on the one hand, and evolutions in business thinking, on the other, contextualising selected business writers and their associated models.

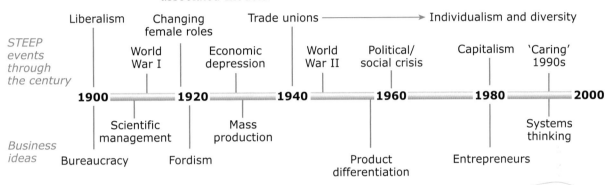

Figure 2.1 The development of business thinking through the last century

1900–50 and World Wars I and II

In the period leading up to World War I and between this and World War II, the UK underwent major changes politically: from having an empire on which 'the sun never set' to losing much of this, hanging on to the remnants as the European political landscape altered dramatically. Political activism grew with, for example, the rise of the trade unions and women being given the vote. Economically speaking, alternate times of boom and bust were critical for business, between the 'roaring twenties' when manufacturing peaked and the depression years of the 1930s before World War II broke out in 1939. Similar events were occurring across Europe and in the USA, the *free markets* of the nineteenth and early twentieth centuries associated with *colonialism* and empire building giving way to protectionism and regulation as industrial nations fought to secure their own interests, literally, politically and economically. (For an explanation of some of the terms used in these sections, refer to your Glossary.)

Business writers and practitioners during this time included Fayol and Taylor who were looking for ways to manage ever growing factories and huge numbers of immigrant workers. Their solutions lay in scientific management to which you were introduced in Book 2, study Session 2. To recap, this involves breaking down each job into its constituent parts and studying productivity with the aim of maximising output. The most famous industrialist of the age, Henry Ford (US pioneer of the first mass produced car, the Model T, mentioned in Book 4) even had this style of business practice named after him: '*Fordism*'.

The Ford Model T car

Influences came not only from political and social changes, but from scientists of the nineteenth and early twentieth centuries whose work had been based on rational, natural science (see section 1.2 in study Session 1) approaches. Writers associated with the period such as **Karl Marx** and **Max Weber**, who wielded their political influences in their work. Weber (1964), for example, considered that the most efficient way of organising a business was along **bureaucratic** lines, that merit and ability to perform an office were far more important than business connections, thus reflecting egalitarian socialist principles.

1950–80: 'you've never had it so good' to the 'winter of discontent'

The way in which business practices were viewed evolved during the 1950s and 1960s, which were decades of economic recovery and prosperity in the UK. Growing academic fields such as psychology and sociology were influential as academics helped business practitioners to understand the needs of their employees and their business in its environment.

This time is also associated with the growing rise of individualism in Western society – of career choice and freedom – as well as with social breakthroughs such as discrimination legislation, the **Women's Movement**, and the **Civil Rights Movement** in the USA. This era gave rise to much debate about equality and rights for all in the workplace.

During this period, there was a trend for very large, conglomerated businesses which could create **economies of scale**, competing on an international basis with diversified products and services. **Expatriation** of employees (that is, working for a subsidiary of a company in another country) became common for large organisations such as BP and Shell and this exposed people to other cultures, influences and ideas, both in business and in social terms. There was also an emphasis on long term strategic planning for coordination and consistency; key to this was thought to be the retention of a motivated, productive and loyal workforce. These influences continued through the 1970s when the economy slumped, and businesses needed as many tools as possible at their disposal to motivate workers. In the UK, this era was characterised by fluctuating relations between employers and trade unions and by political, social and economic unrest. This climate was aggravated by the oil crises and political instability in the Middle East, which made businesses keen to have alternative strategies for survival in reserve.

Vroom's model of expectancy theory, which you studied in Book 2, study Session 2, was developed in 1964 and explicitly linked employee perceptions of management with effort and subsequent reward and, more specifically, spelt out a manager's responsibilities in this process (Vroom, 1964). Models such as Maslow's (1943; 1970), which you also studied in Book 2, study Session 2, continued to be developed, providing business leaders with a pathway to understanding their workers. For example, there is no point in putting on an award-winning educational programme to motivate workers to stay in a company (self-actualisation in Maslow's model of hierarchy) if employees have no coffee machine or lunch break (physiological needs in Maslow's model).

In terms of the wider organisation, **_Burns and Stalker_** (1961) were among the first to categorise organisations within their environment – as 'machines' or 'organisms' – metaphors developed later by Morgan (1986). In brief, a business structured like a machine is suited to stable conditions; an 'organic' business can better cope with instability (see Book 1, study Session 1, section 1.3 to refresh your memory of these terms). This 'contingent' approach took the lessons of the rationalists and evolved them; for instance, it may be appropriate for a stable business, such as a bank or a university, to have a bureaucratic approach (as suggested by Weber, mentioned above); whereas an international fashion house might need fewer rules and greater autonomy so that employees can work more flexibly, responding to constant changes in the market.

The 'entrepreneurial' 1980s, the 'caring' 1990s and beyond

The 1980s onwards saw greater evolution in the way that business was thought about. During the 1980s, in the UK the role of business in society was brought to the forefront by Thatcherite policies (and in the USA by those of Ronald Reagan) which aimed to 'grow' the **_entrepreneurial business model_** that was competitive at the expense of the larger corporations that were seen to be slow moving and bureaucratic. As part of this economic policy, nationalised industries such as gas and telecommunications were sold off to the private sector to improve efficiency and enable them to compete in a free market. Steps were also taken to reduce the power of the trade unions and to promote a more individualistic society.

In this era, Japanese practices were seen to be at the cutting edge of business success, with writers keen to pass on learning on business philosophies such as '**_just-in-time_**', 'total quality management' and **_kaizen_**. This thinking is mirrored in the number of Japanese companies that were welcomed to invest in the UK around this time, particularly in the car industry – Nissan and Toyota, for example. The focus on process, rather than on rules or supervision, adopted by this thinking as a source of advantage was critical to models of business such as Porter's 'five forces model' (Porter, 1990).

Learning from events such as the oil crises of the 1970s, businesses became more aware of their interdependent link with their customers, suppliers, competitors, other industry and the wider environment. They now required business models that could help them understand this complex interaction. The *STEEP* model (which you looked at in Book 1) and Porter's 'five forces model' (mentioned above, and which you looked at in Book 4) were developed during this period. They provide a useful snapshot of what is going on in a business at any one time. The growing turbulence in the business environment, and *boom and bust cycles* in the wider economy, meant that businesses needed to compete by being lean, flexible and responsive. This led to the movements in '*downsizing*' (reducing the number of employees in the business) and '*outsourcing*' (contracting aspects of business out to other companies) of *non-core activities*, and to seeing people as 'human resources' (Book 2).

The present and the future?

Current business writers are looking at a diverse and varied array of business types. At the time of writing (in 2006), there are large, medium, small and micro firms which are all working successfully and competing in the economy. Looking back over the decades since the start of the twentieth century, as we have in this section, it has been relatively easy to pick out a few of the many relevant and useful business models to illustrate the times in which they were written, just as you can pick out pop songs, novels or films that define eras retrospectively. Some models, like the songs, stay in use as they are relevant 'classics'; others become dated and are discarded by business practitioners or are adapted to remain relevant. We hope this section has illustrated that it is necessary to have an understanding of the principal models that have been developed over time in order to decide which models are the most relevant for business today.

That said, it seems likely that the most relevant and useful models today and in the future will develop from issues, trends and debates as they arise both in business and in wider society. We have highlighted three of these below:

- *The debate on **globalisation*** Are our societies and business practices becoming more homogeneous (businesses such as McDonalds and CocaCola with a world presence), or is globalisation creating new fusions of business practices that are different again? This debate reflects not only the way in which Western cultures and political environments are developing – such as moves in the European Union (EU) to widen membership – but also, for example, increasingly international legal responses to current terrorist threats.

- *Technology* Will the internet prove a great leveller and shape the future of all our business dealings? Or will people react against the automation of service and reinvigorate personal business contacts? How will the internet interact with forces for and against globalisation? Again, this reflects the growing social acceptability of the internet, but raises associated issues of security, freedom of information and data protection.

- *Networks* These are currently very much the zeitgeist (the spirit characteristic of an age) of business writings. They have arisen in response to several factors, such as the growth in ***relationship marketing*** at the expense of transaction marketing, and as a way for a business to be flexible and manage quick responses without tying up resources (either assets or people) that are needed for other functions.

2.4 The future: globalisation and corporate power

Let us now reflect for a minute on the current business issues that were raised at the end of the last section. Debates around globalisation rest on whether businesses are becoming more or less alike (in other words, on the extent to which they influence each other), how business should respond to world ***geopolitics*** and external threats, and how institutions (such as the EU) expand and regulate certain countries' economic and business activities. Debates around the impact of technology on business focus on, for instance, whether the internet dispels ***social inequalities of consumption*** (provided everyone has equal access to it), or whether it promotes an increase in the personal **_surveillance_** of consumers. From a critical perspective, there is a common theme throughout all of these debates: power. To become critical scholars of business it is vital that you have an understanding of this central concept and this theme is developed study Session 4.

Activity 2.1

Spend about **30–40 minutes** on this activity

Purpose: to highlight how business has interacted with, and been affected by, its environment over time, and how past events can shape future thinking.

Task: go to the BBC 'On this Day' website (see the Study Companion for the website address), and look at major events that have happened today and on the same date in the year of your birth and the years in which a parent or close friend was born. Then think about the questions below:

1   Which (if any) businesses are featured in the news headlines either on, or around, each day?

2   What other events you looked at might affect, or be affected by, business? (Hint: perhaps try to think of these events in terms of the STEEP framework you used in Book 1.)

3   Do any of these stories in the news fit in with the material you have just read in this study session? If so, how?

Feedback

An example:

For 18 August, two of the main news stories are:

* 1964: South Africa is banned from the Olympics after refusing to condemn apartheid.

* 1969: the end of the Woodstock festival.

Both these stories are relevant to business in some way. For example, companies received bad publicity for importing South African goods, and the Woodstock festival was seen as a landmark in the rise of the new power of young people – and companies began to respond by marketing to this group.

In terms of how this might fit into the material you have just read, the headlines on South Africa and on Woodstock fit into the material on social change and rights for individuals which you read about with regard to the 1960s. Consumers had a choice about whether or not to buy South African oranges, for example, and thus could make their own individual protest against apartheid.

There are no 'right' answers to the a; its purpose has been to help you think about the interaction between business and social and political factors, as indicated in the examples we chose. The headlines you found may also have highlighted technological and environmental factors.

Additionally, we hope it has given you an insight into how major events can help shape perceptions – these might be our own perceptions, or those held by people in business – and how these events might lead a business to make new decisions; for example, to support a development policy, develop strategies to increase employee motivation, or not to export to a country where political beliefs are different from those of the home country.

If you are interested in finding out more about this subject, go to Additional Reading 5.3 in the B120 online resources.

2.5 Conclusion

In this study session we have had a brief look at the social, economic, technical and political forces that have helped to shape business thinking over time and particularly since the beginning of the twentieth century. It is clear that any theories about business, or anything else, will be *embedded* in a particular context. The future will present further challenges to businesses across the world, from which new theories or models are likely to evolve. In the next study session we explore the emergence of globalisation and of multinational corporations.

2.6 Learning outcomes

By the end of this study session on the history of business thinking you should be able to:

- describe some key theories of business and how they have been developed over time;
- outline some of the key business issues of the future.

You will have developed your learning by:

- accessing the BBC website and finding out about some of the news events on particular days such as your birthday;
- enjoying a brief history lesson on business thinking over the last century and the events that shaped this.

Session 3 Globalisation

Why are we studying 'globalisation'? Business a now takes place in the context of instantaneous communication which is without boundaries and operates 24 hours a day, 365 days of the year. This impacts on how businesses are run, how they are structured, where they are located and the influence they may have on national economies.

The **aims and objectives** of Session 3 are to:

- reflect on the meaning of globalisation;
- differentiate between internationalisation and globalisation;
- consider the different drivers of globalisation;
- describe multinational corporations.

3.1 What is globalisation?

The quotation that follows is intended to set the scene for this study session about globalisation and highlight some of the main issues that are inherent within the concept of globalisation:

> Globalization means different things to different people. It can be defined simply as the *expansion of economic activities* across *political boundaries* of *nation states*. More important, perhaps, it refers to a process of *increasing economic openness*, growing *economic interdependence* and deepening *economic integration* between countries in the world economy. It is associated not only with a phenomenal spread and volume of *cross-border economic transactions,* but also with an organization of economic activities which straddles *national boundaries*. This process is driven by the lure of *profit* and the *threat of competition* in the *market.*

> (Nayyar, 2002, p. 200, emphasis added)

Activity 3.1

Spend about **10 minutes** on this activity.

Purpose: to reinforce the definition of globalisation.

Task: we have highlighted some key terms within the quotation above and would like you to reflect on, first, what you think this quotation is about and, second, the meaning of the highlighted terms in the context of the quotation.

Feedback

All the highlighted terms are defined in the Glossary. We wanted you to stop and think for a moment about these key terms associated with globalisation.

We chose the quotation because we thought that, though the author mentions that there is no clear definition of globalisation (it 'means different things to different people'), they give an overall view that, at its simplest, globalisation is about the growth in trade between nations. This growth, which has been exceptional, has been stimulated by firms seeking to make and maintain profits in the face of the demands of international competition. We have drawn attention to the highlighted words because it is important that you understand what these terms mean in the context of globalisation.

Definitions from the Glossary for some of the terms are given below:

- **Nation states**   Discrete countries involved in international trade with other nation states. They may come together to form trade blocs as in, for example, the European Union (comprising twenty-five states at the time of writing (2006)). (See Study Companion for the EU website address.)

- **Increasing economic openness**   Restrictions to trade and to movement of capital and people have been substantially reduced or even eliminated between nation states. This may be seen in the work of the World Trade Organisation (WTO). (If you are interested in finding out more about the WTO, their website address is given in the Study Companion.)

- **Economic interdependence**   Although nation states are discrete entities, trading, financial and political agreements may take place between them, which create relationships of mutual dependency.

- **Integration**   This is the process whereby the growing dependency of nation states on one another means that their economies, resources, firms and policies are more coordinated. In the EU this has been described as **harmonisation.**

- **Profit**   The result when income exceeds expenses for a given period of time. For an individual item the profit is normally the sale proceeds less the costs of acquiring or creating that item.

- **Market**   In marketing terms, the market refers to the actual and potential consumers for a particular product or service. In economic terms, the market is where goods and services are bought and sold.

A further key point about globalisation is that the role of business in the modern economy is now locked into an international system of players who are crucial both as competitors and as partners. There is a difficult and dynamic balance that has to be struck here and we shall examine this later in this study session.

3.2 Internationalisation and globalisation

'Internationalisation' and 'globalisation' are sometimes used interchangeably, but it is possible to differentiate between the two. Boddy (2002, p. 101) helps us to do this through the following examples.

Internationalisation includes activities such as joint ventures with partners in other countries to cooperate in some aspects of business. CocaCola has distribution arrangements with many local companies which promote and distribute their products. The European Airbus is produced by a consortium made up of companies from several countries, which manufacture different parts for assembly at the Aerospatiale factory in Toulouse, France.

Globalisation is an extension of internationalisation in the sense that most aspects of the production or service are performed, and integrated, across many global locations. Boddy uses the example of IBM, a company that has many manufacturing sites across the world which utilise components from many other businesses, which in turn have many sites around the world. This means that customer orders trigger a flow of components through the transport networks (logistics) that link these sites. Thus, national boundaries become more porous and are not the barriers to trade that they once were. This latter point is encouraged by the setting up of trading blocs such as the EU in which the member states have agreed to the eventual removal of many of the obstacles to trade between them and to the creation of a single internal market. The EU has even gone as far as setting up a single currency – the euro – to facilitate this market and the businesses within it (though of course not all member nations have accepted the euro – the UK being an example at the time of writing in 2006).

3.3 Drivers of globalisation

The drivers of globalisation are those pressures or changes that have impelled both businesses and nations to adopt this approach. The different drivers are: cost drivers, market drivers, government drivers and competition drivers. We look at each of these in turn below.

Cost drivers

These seek out an advantage to a business from the possible lowering of the cost of the service or production, and would include:

- gaining *economies of scale* from increasing the size of the business operation;
- the development and growth of technological innovation which simplifies the production process and makes for rapid and extensive communications through the use of information technology (IT) and the internet;
- lower labour and other resource costs in the developing countries found in Africa, India, the Far East and Latin America;
- fast and efficient transportation systems with the development of improved infrastructure.

Market drivers

The development of a world market brings about changes in the demands and tastes of the consumer by:

- the establishment of global brands which have instant recognition and are created and supported by global advertising and marketing (for example, McDonald's fast-food outlets, Nike trainers and sportswear, and Levi jeans); low-cost travel also enables people to purchase consumer goods abroad, thereby reinforcing global brands;
- increasing low-cost travel which begins to create the idea of global consumers with a growing convergence of lifestyles and tastes;

- growing *per capita income*, not only in the developed economies of the West, but in the emerging industrial and services economies; this increases the purchasing power of consumers both individually and organisationally.

Government drivers

Here nations work together to increase the possibility of trading activities in their international trade to create economic advantage and wealth. This can be brought about by:

- a reduction in trade barriers through the removal of tariffs to imports and exports;

- the creation of trading blocs to bring about closer co-operation and economic a between nations; for example, the World Trade Organisation, the EU;

- the creation of more open and freer economies as a result of, for example, the ending of the closed economies of Eastern Europe and the opening up of the Chinese economy; this is a problematic arena as these developments are often linked to an underpinning political agenda which may alter quite rapidly with a change in government or with social instability;

- privatisation of previously centrally controlled industries or organisations: examples include the UK policy of the 1980s and 1990s of selling off to private shareholders previous state monopolies such as gas, telecommunications and electricity, and more recently in Russia of selling off the oil industry. The idea behind this is that release from state influence will enable the new organisations to operate along more businesslike lines and seek out new markets and suppliers, driven by the profit motive.

Competition drivers

The opening up of economies or businesses creates an environment in which more players can enter the marketplace, whether nationally or internationally. This means that competition will increase as the businesses strive to attract potential consumers for their products or services both at home and overseas. This is brought about by:

- the cross-border ownership of home firms by foreign organisations; for example, Rupert Murdoch's USA–based News International Group's ownership of key media organisations in the UK, such as the *Times* and *Sun* newspapers and Sky TV;

- movement of companies to become globally centred rather than nationally centred through acquisition, strategic alliances and takeover;

- the growth of these global networks of organisational structures and businesses which make countries interdependent within specific industries; for example, the European Airbus project mentioned earlier.

Underpinning many of the points listed above is the growth in international financial markets, which means that close financial relationships are established on a worldwide basis which facilitate a complex and sophisticated international system of lending, borrowing, transmission and storage of money. This is aided by supranational financial organisations such as the World Bank and the International Monetary Fund (IMF). (If you are interested in finding out more about the IMF, you will find the website address in the Study Companion.)

Having looked at some of the reasons why globalisation has emerged on such a scale, we now need look at the advantages and disadvantages that it might bring. To help you reflect on this, we would like you to complete the following short a. You should be able to use your experience and existing knowledge gained from your general reading, watching the television news and talking with friends or colleagues, or perhaps from being a member of a pressure group or working in a business.

Activity 3.2

Spend about **15 minutes** on this activity.

Purpose: to consider the positive and negative aspects of the growth of globalisation in business.

Task: make a list of what you consider to be the possible advantages and disadvantages of globalisation.

Feedback

Your list could have included some or all of the following possible advantages and disadvantages of globalisation:

Advantages:

- Globalisation generates wealth, goods and services which are now available to a greater percentage of the world's population.
- It gives rise to economies of scale (the more you produce the cheaper it becomes) in the production process, which drive down average costs, resulting in cheaper products.
- Businesses are better able to seek out low-cost producers and move the manufacture of goods and the provision of services to these, resulting in more competitive prices for products and services.
- Globalisation increases the potential market for goods and services.
- It facilitates growth in communications – the internet, email, satellite television – which enables direct access to news, events and education and can undermine the ability of authoritarian nations to keep their populations ignorant.

Disadvantages:

- The vast majority of the world's population may not be able to purchase these consumer goods, even at the lower prices.
- The new technologies and access to communications may not benefit all in that they create social and economic desires which cannot be met within all societies. This may undermine the nature of a society and destabilise it.

- The products of the global economy may destroy the manufacturing diversity and cultural heritage of a country as products become standardised worldwide.

- The enhanced production of goods and services may have an environmental cost in terms of depletion of natural resources, waste and pollution which ultimately will outweigh the benefits – think, for example, of the growth in the world car market, the emission of carbon dioxide and links to global warming.

- Globalisation may undermine the idea of the nation state as a global business becomes more powerful – financially and politically – than its host country.

It should be clear from these lists of possible advantages and disadvantages that the arena of globalisation is not value free and that there is a variety of perspectives from which it can be approached. Often these approaches are locked into a political agenda which will further confuse the issue as a particular 'spin' will be put on the ideas in an attempt to support or refute arguments. There is, in fact, no easy answer as to whether globalisation is a good or a bad thing, but it remains a fact of modern business life. The concept of globalisation will need close and ongoing examination to ensure its relevance and place as businesses are further driven by the growth in world competition and as they search for worldwide cost and resource advantages. We can see this taking place with the outsourcing of production and services by organisations such as British Telecom (BT) which move call centres to the Indian subcontinent, or Nike whose trainers are manufactured in the Far East. Both of these businesses are what we would define as **_multinational corporations_** (MNCs).

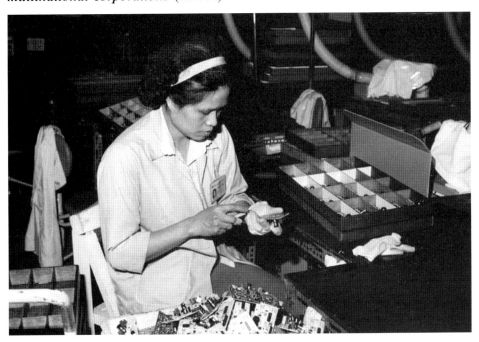

Outsourcing of production in the Far East is a feature of globalisation

3.4 Multinational corporations

The largest businesses in the global economy tend to be the multinational corporations (MNCs). Many of these are household names, producing services and products with which we are all familiar. Put simply, an MNC is a business that has invested in several countries, has employees in these countries and whose products and services are marketed on a worldwide basis. Increasingly, MNCs are working in such a way that, while they maintain their centralised control over key issues such as strategy, research and development from the parent country, they often give a high degree of autonomy to a national subsidiary over such things as sourcing raw materials, local employment practices and manufacturing. An example of this is the US company Nike which produces trainers and sportswear: while the technological skills and knowledge (high-level skills) remain within the parent business in the USA, the more routine aspects (low-level skills) of the business have been sent outside the home economy to low-cost countries.

Multinational corporations are large businesses that have budgets which involve sums of money that are often larger than the **_gross domestic product_** (GDP) of the nations with which they are involved. (For example, in 2004, eBay sold 1.4 billion items worth $34.2 billion. If sales were GDP, eBay would be the southern hemisphere's tenth largest nation, just behind Peru and ahead of Ecuador: Wyss, 2005.) This gives them significant power with governments and world institutions both at a national and at an international level. They also have a significant impact on the structuring of local economies and on both job creation and the nature of the jobs created. In addition, it can also be suggested that MNCs exploit and dominate consumers, their local communities and the natural environment (Sloman and Sutcliffe, 2000).

Multinational corporations hold significant economic power. They control a large proportion of the world's economic assets and resources, such as raw materials, production facilities or financial resources. This economic power gives these businesses a great deal of influence over people and other types of businesses and institutions. If a business controls important natural resources, it may use this as a bargaining tool to obtain higher prices and other concessions from other businesses which need these resources. This is easier to do in times of high unemployment than in times of worker shortages, when trade unions or government agencies concerned with employee welfare have a stronger bargaining position. Businesses can also use any control of scarce or particularly desirable goods and services to gain higher prices. Again, they will be more successful in this when there is high demand for these goods and services. In times of economic depression the bargaining power of businesses vis-à-vis their customers are reduced.

This economic power tends to give business a significant amount of political power. Most governments want to promote stable and prosperous economic conditions and are thus happy to support business activity which leads to such outcomes. Business therefore often has considerable influence over government policy and legislation. It may use this influence to lobby governmental and other political agents for favourable legislation and relaxed regulation (for instance, in terms of less employee, consumer or environmental protection), lower taxes, or other policy measures that favour business (such as government-sponsored training). In order to increase their political bargaining power, individual businesses tend to organise themselves into business and trade associations, which lobby government and other *stakeholders* on behalf of their members.

If you are interested in finding out more about the ethics of global business, you might like to look at Additional Readings 5.4 and 5.5 in the B120 online resources.

The final activity in this study session will give you an insight into just how 'global' many everyday products are.

Activity 3.3

Spend about **30 minutes** on this activity.

Purpose: to demonstrate how 'global' everyday products are.

Task: see whether you can find any 'global' products in your home. You may be able to identify some of them by the fact that the information they have on them will be in more than one language. This means that the same item is designed to be distributed in more than one market – a strategy of global integration.

Feedback

One member of the B120 course team found the following:

- Pears soap, which is sold by a British company. The bar was made under licence in India.

- Clinique face lotion, made by an American company (originally French). The product was made in the UK and information given in American English, French, German, Spanish and Italian.

- Lindt chocolate: Lindt is a Swiss company, but the product was made in France. The information was given in English, Spanish, Portuguese, Finnish, Danish, Swedish and Polish. Names of distributors in the UK, Spain, Australia, Colombia, Brazil, Portugal, Finland, Denmark Poland were listed.

- Epson colour inkjet printer, made by a Japanese company and marketed in the USA, the UK, Germany, France, Australia, Singapore, Hong Kong, Taiwan, Italy, Spain, Portugal and Japan. The brochure was written in English, German, French, Italian and Spanish.

- IBM software: IBM is an American company. The licence agreement was in the following languages: English, Chinese, Japanese, Danish, Dutch, Finnish, French, German, Italian, Norwegian, Portuguese, Spanish, Russian, Swedish and two others we weren't able to identify.

You may also have found items (multinational products) that seemed to have been produced for one particular market, but from the language on the labels you could tell that it was not aimed at your own country (as if you had bought it while you were on holiday abroad). Such products are often cut-price, which suggests that there are businesses that can make a living transferring multinational products from one part of the world to another, taking advantage perhaps of different price levels in different economies.

3.5 Conclusion

Globalisation has a number of powerful drivers and bestows advantages and disadvantages on different nations and regions within the world economy. However, globalisation also involves an accumulation of power and dominance for capitalist organisations, sometimes rendering them more economically powerful than the nations in which they are located. Because of the pervasive nature of the disadvantages of globalisation, various networks, organisations and perspectives which question and resist the basis of global corporate power have grown since the 1970s. Individuals, groups, organisations such as trade unions and non-governmental organisations, and governments seek to limit or regulate some of the more problematic and difficult consequences of business activity. In the next two study sessions we endeavour to illustrate this through a discussion of power. In study Session 4, we discuss the concept and the dimensions of power as these relate to business. In study Session 5, we look at resistance to and ways of challenging the power of business.

3.6 Learning outcomes

By the end of this study session on globalisation you should be able to:

- define the term 'globalisation';
- differentiate between internationalisation and globalisation;
- describe possible advantages and disadvantages of globalisation;
- explain the place and power of multinational corporations in business.

You will have developed your learning by:

- possibly accessing the International Monetary Fund website to understand more about international financial organisations;
- exploring the 'global-ness' of products in your home.

Session 4 Business and power

Why are we studying 'business and power'? A central element of being able to critique modern business practices at any level of analysis is to have a grasp of how power works, not only within organisations, but between organisations and within societies as a whole.

The **aims and objectives** of Session 4 are to:

- outline and explain the three dimensions of power;
- explain how power works at multiple levels;
- explain how power is associated not only with overt conflict, but also with the culture and structure of organisations and societies;
- explore these ideas in the analysis of an article.

4.1 Power and influence

This study session begins to explore power in relation to business. Let us begin by returning to three issues introduced in the last study two study sessions. These are:

1 *Globalisation* Whether businesses across the globe become more alike over time depends on whether one particular business model for a particular sector influences managers within other businesses to comply with it. Managers' abilities to redesign their businesses require local influencing and political skills to win over the opposition.

2 *Technology* Similarly, responding to geopolitical world events requires an assessment of the actual threat of those events occurring – powerful threats will cause managers to design and implement new systems (for example, security and access control systems) to protect their business.

3 *Networks* The claim that the internet dispels social inequalities assumes that each person who wants to conduct business or consume using the internet has access to it. Frequently, having access to the internet relies not only on our economic buying power to equip ourselves with a computer, but also our time resources, skills and social space to surf the Web. In addition, the amount of ***personal information*** gathered through internet retailing programs feeds into the relationship marketing of a business and provides a massive net benefit through the sale of databases and ***customer profiling***, with little benefit for the consumer who (perhaps inadvertently) has provided the business with the details of their personal preferences.

Each one of these examples involves an exercise of power, control and influence by one individual, group, business or institution over another.

A central element of being able to critique modern business practices at any level of analysis is to have a grasp of how power works, not only within a business but between businesses and within societies as a whole. Power is a very complex phenomenon, but, if we reflect on all the concepts we have explored in this book so far (including levels of analysis, epistemology, reification and ontology), things will become clearer.

4.2 The dimensions of power

Power, in the human context, has long been recognised as the ability to make someone do what they otherwise would not, and is not a simple matter of coercion. It is easy for the owner of a business to exercise power over a group of employees to get them to carry out their work for the business because the owner rewards them with money. But if skilled employees are in short supply, they can exercise power over the owner by bargaining for higher wages because they are scarce. You may be familiar with the term '*empowerment*'. In business we talk about various individuals, groups and organisations being 'empowered' in particular situations when they are able to complete meaningful tasks when they choose to, with competence and choice, and observe the impacts of their actions. Empowered organisational members have access to the resources they need to achieve their objectives. Because of the complexity of organisations, on a daytoday basis it is very difficult to pin down who or what has power, is empowered or lacks power in any definitive or permanent sense. The ground is constantly shifting. In order to appreciate its nature, complexity and effects, it is most accurate to review power as operating at a number of levels.

Power has three dimensions (Watson, 2001, pp. 322–3):

1   an interpersonal dimension;

2   an organisational–structural–cultural dimension;

3   a societal–structural–cultural dimension.

These are sometimes referred to as 'faces' of power. Let us now explore these in greater detail.

The interpersonal dimension, or the first face of power

The first face of power, which is perhaps the simplest, draws on the work of Dahl (1957). The basic idea is this: A has power over B to the extent that A can get B to do something they wouldn't otherwise do.

In other words, I might not want to do a particular job for you, such as clean your shoes or write your computer programs, but I do so because you are bigger than me, or you persuade me to do so with offers of untold riches. In the first face of power, there is some observable disagreement or conflict at an *interpersonal level.*

The organisational–structural–cultural dimension, or the second face of power

The second face of power builds on the first. The first face was based on actions or events that actually take place, but what about events that don't take place? What makes things not reach the agenda? Who rules these out as unimportant? This is also an issue of power; that is, the power to determine what is discussed, and what isn't. The work of Dahl looked only at decisions

– actual events – but what happens the rest of the time? What happens, for instance, to issues or groups of people who never get to the decision making arena?

Hence, the second face of power refers to the pattern of relationships within an organisation such as a business whereby rules, hierarchy and cultural norms (to which people have 'signed up' by joining the business) make it normal and reasonable for some people to get others to do what they otherwise wouldn't do. It is the existence of this second level of power that makes it possible for the boss to actually ask you the question: 'will you clean my shoes?', or 'will you write my computer program?' There is a hidden agenda in businesses which says that people further up the hierarchy, who have a higher status because of that hierarchy, can ask people lower down to do jobs for them; or that certain business functions or departments have a greater influence on matters than others.

The societal–structural–cultural dimension of power, or the third face of power

The third dimension of power is the most radical and is probably the most difficult to grasp. It concerns the pattern of relationships and understandings generally prevailing in a society at large, and how power is distributed throughout that society. This means, first, that certain groups, or sectors of society, have the material capacity to exert pressure on others (because they have wealth, access to policy arenas, membership of particular networks and institutions, and so on), and, second, that a *legitimacy* is given to practices whereby certain people get others to do what they would not otherwise do. The practice of ordering people about on a large scale becomes normal, so that whole sections of society are more or less subordinated to others and it is accepted that they are.

Many current societies incorporate a particular system of ownership and wealth. These societies also incorporate business institutions whose managers administer some of that wealth on the owners' behalves. This means that, as a manager, you can, under certain conditions, offer me money to write your computer programs or clean your shoes. In other words, the culture in which we live identifies some people as managers and some as workers. Watson defined power as: 'The capacity of an individual or group to affect the outcome of any situation so that access is achieved to whatever resources are scarce and desired within a society or a part of that society' (Watson, 2002, p. 323).

Although there are three different dimensions of power, there is one underlying theme: individuals, or groups of people, have a certain capacity to affect outcomes to their advantage. These outcomes relate to how particular goods or resources are valued in society, and distributed throughout it. Without scarcity of resources there would be no need to exert power, and even when power is exerted between two individuals in private, it is impossible to separate that 'transaction' from the culture, structure and patterns of advantage and disadvantage in the society to which those individuals belong.

So how do we go about applying all these concepts of power to help us think more critically about business? Read the following Case Study and complete Activity 4.1 following it to help you do this (take a look at the task for Activity 4.1 before you read the case study).

Case Study 4.1

Re-engineering the Doocot

Dovecot Components has been an important employer in this town for a long time. Most people around here just call it 'The Doocot'. For over twenty years now the workforce has been steadily falling as we have increased investment in newer technologies and found a whole lot of ways of making the work less labour intensive. Productivity was steadily rising over this period and, as a management, we felt freer to make changes without having to fight with trade unions over every little detail. Government policies were partly responsible for this, but the unions – indeed the workforce generally – recognised that we were struggling in an increasing difficult and increasingly international market place. Almost every year would see some redundancies and there was not a great deal of argument about this. I think people regarded these job losses as a sort of unfortunate fact of life and I don't think they affected morale within the company to any real extent. But people did not realise just how difficult things were going to get as we saw the auto companies that bought our components increasingly looking across the whole global economy to source their production.

About five years ago we realised that we needed to make radical changes in the business. We had been developing our technologies incrementally over the years and had introduced at different times a variety of innovations ranging from quality improvement groups to cellular and team working. A lot of our production is now done on a just-in-time basis. Components go out of the door just a few hours before the car plant two hundred miles away needs them to stick in its cars. It was becoming clear to us, however, that there were increasing numbers of other suppliers who could get their products to the factories just as promptly. And not only could they supply at significantly lower prices but several of them were much faster than us at developing and improving their products. Our customers were facing increasing global competition just as we were and were constantly looking to improve the quality and functionality of the components they put in their vehicles.

At the first executive meetings where we talked seriously about making radical changes I put forward a plan to set up a completely new 'Research, Design and Manufacturing Innovation' department. This would be a crack team that I would recruit by head hunting from my quite extensive contacts across the engineering world. It would combine product development and the improving of production methods – making sure we designed for ease of manufacture as well as to delight our customers. Immediately I suggested this I was shot down. The first bloke to 'have a go' didn't bother me. As a management accountant, our finance man was right to look critically at my plans and question how we could possibly afford this. But, like everyone else, I knew that he personally disliked me and would attack anything I put forward. It was the MD, Jerry Penick, who really put the boot in however. This did bother me. In the first place, he said, 'there is certainly no way we can afford to do that'. And, 'secondly', he went on, 'your whole philosophy is out of date'. That made me wild. I ranted on about how advanced my 'design for manufacturing' ideas were and that I would easily get a job with one of our competitors if he had so little respect for me. In fact I did slam out of the meeting at one point. I think it was when the manufacturing director – a blinkered and territorially minded idiot if ever there was one – made it clear that he wasn't keen for me to get involved in manufacturing issues. The MD came and found me puffing a cigar in the directors' lavatory and persuaded me to go back into the meeting and hear his thoughts on 're-engineering the Doocot'.

It turned out that the consultants that Jerry had brought in six months earlier, 'just to look over things' as he told us, had in fact come up with this scheme to 're-engineer' the processes in Doocot 'from top to bottom'. 'We have got to jump out of our functional boxes and our obsession with departmental boundaries', he said, looking directly at me and then at my manufacturing colleague. 'Everything has got to be stripped down to the basics and everyone will make their contribution to the basic processes of getting ideas quickly and efficiently through from the drawing board to the customer's delivery bay. The bloke on the drawing board will be as interested in that customer's needs as the driver of the delivery wagon will – or as I will'.

At this stage we were all looking at each other a little shocked. Most of us had heard of this 'business re-engineering' thing, but had not really related it to our situation. Molly, our marketing woman, ventured to say that all the re-engineering cases that she had come across had been more exercises in 'blood letting' and 'axing people as well as departments' than improving processes. 'Well', came back Jerry, 'I don't want any talk like that. But the re-engineering exercise will mean taking quite a big axe to our management structures. Levels will be taken out.' He accepted that 'delayering' and 'becoming leaner' would be painful. The consultants, together with a small senior management team, would 'look at everybody's job' and nobody 'whose job doesn't serve our core processes' would survive. This would be hard and it would 'hurt everybody involved', Jerry said. But those who survived would be much better off. It wasn't just that their jobs would be more secure. Their 'prospects with the firm' would also be better. Above all, people would benefit by being 'more empowered'. He explained that, at present, all the efforts that people put in and all the operations across the plant had to be 'made to add up' by managers, supervisors and other 'functionaries'. By taking a lot of these out, people would be given the satisfaction of 'adding it all up' for themselves. And, he added, by 'taking away all the managerial buffers that exist between the workforce and the market place' people will see the need to 'work hard, conscientiously and cooperatively *for the business and not for their department* because they will know that if they don't we all go under'.

The whole thing seemed sensible, if rather terrifying. For six months the 'Re-engineering Action Group' (RAG), comprising four senior managers and four consultants, were to work 'day and night' with Jerry to 'completely reshape the business'. The business was to be more 'focused' than at present and this basically meant making it smaller. 'We have got too big and unwieldy', Jerry argued, 'so we'll cut the less profitable lines and try to stay at a size where a smallish top management team can keep their eyes on everything'. There would be a major investment in ICT, with the savings made on labour costs more than covering the 'costs of the new computer systems'. The 'software and hardware that are available now for management control', he insisted, 'were sophisticated enough now to cover the work of all the people who will be leaving us – and more'.

So, all of this went ahead. I was lucky to be kept on. But both my finance director and manufacturing director colleagues – and enemies – got the push. I was on the RAG – the action group charged with 'implementing' the re-engineering. At first I felt privileged. But this feeling soon went. I began to realise quite early on that the whole thing was doomed from the start. We had embraced business process re-engineering in a big way. But we had embraced a monster. In principle, I thought, it was wise. It was harsh. But harsh measures were necessary. And all of those who stayed with the business would experience a much higher level of empowerment and involvement with the core processes of the enterprise. They would clearly benefit. But as we all quickly learned, it wasn't to happen like that, and it's so easy to see why, in retrospect.

In one voice, we were saying that people were to be empowered, to be trusted and were to have their 'energies' released to do 'really meaningful work'. But in another voice we were asking people to kneel down to have their heads chopped off. This is where the massive catch in the whole thing lay. On the one hand we were asking people to be empowered, to manage themselves and be committed to the business. The logic of de-layering was one of saying that an empowered and committed workforce could, in many respects, manage things better than managers could. But on the other hand, we were a group of managers and consultants acting as if we were mighty gods who knew better than anyone how things should be done.

As you can imagine, the whole thing was treated with deep suspicion and bitter hostility from the beginning. And that's just among the managers! We RAG members were treated with utter disdain and mistrust as hypocrites and axe wielders. Because nobody would cooperate with us or give us any information we could trust, we simply could not do the work we were meant to do. But how could we back down? Consequently we made lots of cuts and we reorganised the place from top to bottom without really knowing what we were doing. And, yes, the business has survived. But we are running it through a regime of terror with most of the best staff we had having moved out to other jobs. I give the business a couple more years at the most. And I shall be out of here well before that. When you see me next time, I'll have flown the Doocot.

(Source: Watson, 2002, pp. 315–18)

Activity 4.1

Spend about **40 minutes** on this activity.

Purpose: to identify the different 'faces' of power through a case study.

Task: read Roberto Auldearn's account in Case Study 4.1. As you do so, note down the different faces of power you spot in the case study. Give an example of each face of power, how it works and who or what it affects.

Feedback

The boardroom events that Roberto Auldearn told us about involved interpersonal power rivalries between Roberto and two other senior managers. There seemed in this to be elements of both material interests ('territoriality') and emotions (personal dislikes are mentioned). Also at this level, we see Jerry Penick very clearly wielding power over all the other managers. He is exerting his authority as the managing director of the company – not just to 'put the boot in' to Roberto's ideas or to say who will and will not be involved in the 'action group'. He actually sacks the manufacturing and the finance directors. Jerry's use of his chief executive's authority to act towards these individuals in this way is connected to the interpersonal dimension and to the organisational-structural-cultural dimension of the power that is operating here. And that dimension would not exist unless it, in turn, was embedded in a set of cultural institutions and wealth ownership patterns at the societal level that gives chief executives the right to act in this way.

However, Jerry's power behaviour with regard to the re-engineering of the business also has to be understood in the light of the global changes in the way wealth and power is being restructured in an increasingly international marketplace. The power relationships between major corporations are shifting. And formal governmental politics are also playing a part in the power plays occurring in Dovecot Components, as Roberto's mention of government industrial relations policies suggests. However, the outcomes of all of this go way beyond the boardroom. The access to scarce and valued resources of all of those who lose their jobs as a result of the restructuring of Dovecote will be seriously affected. Power and politics in the board rooms of work organisations create winners and losers both within those boardrooms and in the communities within which the organisations are located. '***Micropolitics***' must always be understood in the context of '***macropolitics***'.

Reproduced in Example 4.1 below is part of an article from *The Economist* of 8 September 2005, which focuses on the Indian economy and the influence on this of the outsourcing of work from multinational companies. Your reflection on this example forms the basis of the following activity.

Example 4.1

The last thing you would expect India's call-centre bosses to be worrying about is a shortage of staff. The entire 'business process outsourcing' (BPO) industry, including a wide range of services besides manning [sic] the telephone, employs an estimated 348,000 people … . Nearly 3m[illion] English speakers graduate from university every year. That has been India's big attraction: call-centres have been spoilt for choice. Yet finding and retaining qualified workers has become the industry's biggest medium-term worry. It may, as a new report by Gartner, a consultancy, puts it 'stall the offshore call-centre boom'.

The infant industry has grown explosively. Youngsters have hopped from job to job. Staff-attrition rates for the industry as a whole have climbed to 45–50% a year. Entry-level salaries have now reached about 10,000 rupees a month ($230), considered very high for a first job (which explains why outsourcing to India remains so attractive). Training costs are also mounting, as firms take on less-qualified applicants. Sam Chopra, president of the Call Centre Association of India (CCAI), which represents some 60 of India's 400-odd BPO firms, says the pressure is such that firms do not always check staff references at once. Such slipshod practices are blamed for the very few, but widely publicised, fraud scandals.

Call-centre jobs, rather glamorous until recently, are losing their allure. Staff often have to work nights, put up with abuse and undergo undignified security checks. With the number of BPO workers expected to reach 1m[illion] by 2009, a shortfall of 260,000 qualified personnel is predicted. Sujay Chohan, of Gartner, contrasts BPO with India's booming software-development industry. There, Indian firms grew in parallel with their mostly American clients. Engineering colleges, in-house trainers and private institutes kept pace with demand. In businesses such as call-centres, however, growth is even faster and training has been much less organised.

The industry is beginning to help itself. The CCAI, with the Confederation of Indian Industry, has launched a training initiative. It will offer a standardised qualification for new BPO workers: improving English, 'neutralising' accents, teaching some computer skills and so on. NASSCOM, a lobby for the software and services industry, is also introducing an 'assessment and certification' programme for would-be employees. Such schemes should cut costs, ease wage pressures and help keep crooks out.

India still has a unique combination of manpower [sic] and English-language skills. But the full potential of BPO, beyond call-centres, has only been glimpsed – there are huge emerging markets in legal services, accounting, health care, personnel services, and so on. It would be a shame if India were to miss out by misusing its one unbeatable, seemingly inexhaustible resource: well-educated young people.

(Source: *Economist,* 2005, p. 60)

Activity 4.2

Spend about **40 minutes** on this activity.

Purpose: to reinforce your understanding of the faces of power in the context of the influence of the outsourcing of work from multinational companies on the Indian economy.

Task: reread Example 4.1. Again, note down as you do so the different faces of power you spot. Give an example of each face of power, how it works and who or what it affects.

Feedback

The article illustrates the complexities of power relationships associated with the callcentre industry in India. A number of levels can be identified: first, the experience of the individual worker; second, the experiences of the call centres themselves; and third, the experience of the whole business process outsourcing, or BPO, industry and the institutions which govern it.

The first face of power (interpersonal) is illustrated by the discussion of workers' experiences: having to undergo security checks under the threat of not getting a job; having to take abuse from customers and work unsociable hours is disempowering. However, they are simultaneously empowered within the wider economy because they are relatively highly paid. Individual and collective fraudsters had some power over the industry by threatening data security.

The second face of power (organisational–structural–cultural) is illustrated through the desperate practices of call centres in trying to fill their vacancies. Because of high attrition rates and the pressure of the market, the call centres themselves are disempowered, and norms of being slipshod with their training and recruitment practices are seen to be emerging. Industry-level regulation is involved in the establishment of new controls over the human resource aspect of the BPO industry, which might generate conflict or inertia when the new norms and controls begin to supplant the older ones.

The third face of power, concerning the Indian society as a whole, is referred to at the very end of the article. India has been keen to market itself internationally as an outsourcing destination of choice for overseas multinationals. In doing so, however, the norms the country is trying to generate and establish – about having a skilled population – could be undermined.

4.3 Conclusion

Having considered some basic concepts and explored them with an example, there are several things about the nature of power that should now be clear. First, it is not a static entity – it is complex and works at many levels. We are all engaged in power relationships of some kind, and frequently, because of the many relationships that we have with our colleagues, friends, families and businesses of which we are part, we experience different intensities and kinds of power simultaneously. Moreover, because of our widespread engagement in these relationships, understanding power is often about understanding difference – differences in opinion, norms, culture and structure between settings. Hence, while understanding why we comply is essential to understanding power, so is understanding why we don't: in other words, why resistance and conflict occur. In the next study session we introduce some of the ways in which the power of business might be resisted.

4.4 Learning outcomes

By the end of this study session on business and power you should be able to:

- describe the theory of the three faces of power and explain its relevance to studying business;
- appreciate the complexity of power.

You will have developed your learning by:

- working through a case study and an example which explore how power works in business.

Session 5 Resisting and challenging business power

Why are we studying 'resisting and challenging business power'? As part of our exploration of critical and alternative views of business, we have so far established, through a discussion of globalisation, that multinational corporations and business in general are powerful in shaping national economies and regions. However, as we are also keen to explore resistance and difference as an aspect of power, we are now going to examine how globalisation and corporate power is resisted at a number of different levels.

The **aims and objectives** of Session 5 are to:

- outline how corporate power affects the lives of ordinary people as citizens and employees;
- outline the different ways in which corporate power can be resisted and challenged;
- apply these ideas to a case study.

5.1 Negative business power

In the other books on this course we have treated business as the generally useful and positive a that it often is. However, there is a 'dark side' to business in that businesses can sometimes act in ways which are not necessarily in the interest of the wider social good. While we are not suggesting here that this is always the case, or that negative aspects of business a are necessarily due to the bad intentions of business owners and managers, this 'dark side' of business is sufficiently important that you should spend a little time learning and thinking about it. This is the purpose of this section.

Business (both business as a whole and some individual businesses) has a lot of power within both the national and the global context, the power to achieve many positive things but also the power to do harm. It is an important part of a rounded understanding of business to be aware of these issues. There are also two reasons why, as an individual, you might want to understand them:

1   As a citizen, you will at times be affected by this power, probably both in positive and negative ways, and it is in your interest to know about and recognise it in its various forms and to understand how it might be controlled or balanced.

2   As a (potential) business leader, or even an employee, you may at some point be in the position to wield some of this power and need to be able to do so critically and responsibly.

Activity 5.1

Spend about **10 minutes** on this activity.

Purpose: to start thinking about the influence that business has over your own life.

Task: think of two instances – one positive, one negative – where the power of business has affected you or someone you know.

Feedback

Positive examples may include being given a job; a business providing a good or service that was really important; or perhaps a business donating money to a charitable cause that is important to you. Negative examples could include losing or not getting a particular job; not getting goods or services needed: for instance, living in an area where there are no shops (a 'food desert' in an inner city area might be an example of this); being affected by noise or pollution from a factory, and so on.

While businesses undoubtedly have a lot of power in various forms and can sometimes be found to be exploiting it, their power does not necessarily go unchallenged. There are several possible ways in which business power can be controlled. You should now spend a little time thinking about how this might be done.

Activity 5.2

Spend about **10 minutes** on this activity.

Purpose: to start thinking about possible controls on the power of business.

Task: make a (short) list of people or institutions that you think might play a role in controlling business power. For each of these, give an example of the kind of control over business they might exert.

Feedback

You are likely to have identified a number of different individuals, groups of people or institutions. The main ways in which business power can be controlled are discussed in the next section.

5.2 Controlling business power

The main ways in which business power might be controlled are:

- voluntary action on the part of businesses
- government regulation
- consumer action
- direct action of pressure groups.

These are now discussed in more detail.

Voluntary action on the part of businesses

We have already looked at **business ethics** earlier in the course (for example, Book 1, study Session 5 and Book 4, study Sessions 2–4). Ethics in this context refers to businesses conducting their activities in accordance with generally accepted ethical norms. From this derives the idea of **corporate social responsibility** (CSR); that is, that businesses need to take responsibility for the social consequences of their actions and try to minimise and mitigate negative consequences as much as possible. It has been argued that CSR can have various benefits for businesses themselves, in addition to benefits for stakeholders and society at large. Businesses with a good social image may find it easier to attract high-quality employees; customers may like their responsible stance and prefer to buy from them; and other stakeholders may also lend their support, which may lead to a more positive treatment by government agencies and regulators. This in turn can lead to reduced costs, as the business is less likely to face legal claims for example, and to improved profits due to better performance by employees and increased sales. Thus, good CSR is thought to lead to enhanced financial performance (Waddock and Graves, 1997).

However, if customers or stakeholders were *not* concerned with the social performance of business, CSR would be unlikely to pay off for businesses and they would be unlikely to take an interest in it. The actions of these stakeholders are therefore highly important. This is because, particularly since the 1980s, there have been several high-profile examples of how the market mechanism does not always provide the information and warning signals that shareholders and stakeholders expect. The Maxwell Communications, BCCI, Polly Peck, Enron, Worldcom, Global Crossing and Parmalat scandals revealed that auditing procedures alone were insufficient in ensuring responsible corporate governance. In short, voluntary action on the part of the business may be unlikely to happen in the absence of government, customer and/or stakeholder concern.

Government regulation

Government regulation is often considered the main form of external control of businesses. Business is subject to numerous laws, relating to issues ranging from the legal form business enterprises may take; how they account for their finances; how they deal with employees, consumers and other stakeholders; to their impact on the natural environment. These laws are often enforced through specific regulatory agencies, such as the **Environment Agency** in the UK. Such regulation of business by government exists everywhere, even in countries where the official rhetoric is one of little state intervention in business affairs. There is, however, some variation in the extent of business-related legislation in different countries and, crucially, the extent to which such legislation is actually enforced. These differences are to some degree due to differences in political systems and ideology, but more than anything else they are due to the resources that the government in a country commands. This is the reason why there is often significantly less enforcement of business regulation in poor countries, giving businesses operating in them proportionally greater power to act as they see fit. Abuses of power, for which multinational corporations are often criticised, can happen much more easily in countries with weak governments.

Consumer action

Another avenue of controlling business power is through consumer action. Increasing numbers of consumers want not only to buy products that are of high quality, stylish, durable, and so on, but also to buy from businesses that act in socially responsible ways. Consumers can take two forms of action to influence companies:

1   They can boycott products they consider to be unethical in some ways (for example, animal furs) or that are made by businesses they consider to act in irresponsible ways (for instance, those that have a bad human rights or environmental record).

2   They can actively seek out products and companies with a positive ethical image (for example, the Fairtrade range of coffee).

Sometimes these consumer actions have shown considerable influence in shaping business behaviour. For instance, consumer boycotts in Europe effectively eliminated the trade in baby seal furs, and hence the killing of seals, in the 1980s. In the UK, consumers have shown great interest in buying fairly traded products and the market for these has expanded greatly in recent years. However, as Klein (2001) points out, consumer action will normally affect only those companies whose products and activities are very visible in the market. Consumers have little influence over relatively unknown companies or those that don't sell to consumers at all.

Direct action of pressure groups

Pressure groups are a further monitor and influence on business power. They work in several different ways to influence business behaviour. They appeal to citizens and consumers, making questionable business activities known and hoping to influence citizens either to demand government action or to take action themselves in the kinds of ways described above. They also lobby government to take policy action that will control business power. For instance, environmental groups respond to government consultations and approach government with requests and proposals, making the case for legislation that protects the environment, often against shortterm business interests. Increasingly, pressure groups also work directly with businesses, perhaps by working in partnership with businesses that have shown an interest in taking responsibility for the social and environmental consequences of their activities.

Often pressure groups (for example, Greenpeace) employ tactics that will gain media attention, thereby hoping to make their case to both citizens and policy makers. This direct action can be either confrontational or constructive. Confrontational action might involve, for example, protesting outside the headquarters of a business, sabotage (the damaging of industrial equipment) and road blocks.

There is no single, perfect solution to the control of business power. A mixture of voluntary, responsible action by businesses themselves, government control, consumer interest and scrutiny by pressure groups and the media is most likely to result in a situation of adequate checks and balances, where business contributes positively to economic development and makes a profit for its owners, without causing too many negative social and environmental side effects.

If you are interested in finding out more about controlling business power, you might like to look at Additional Reading 5.6 in the B120 online resources.

We will now explore the issues raised in this section through a case study about the flawed decision made by Ford in the 1970s to build the Pinto in a way which could be fatal to its occupants in the event of a crash. Before reading the case study, take a look at the task for Activity 5.3 which follows it.

Case Study 5.1

Death in the Ford Motor Company balance sheet

In August 1970, the Ford Motor Company launched its latest car – the Pinto – onto the US market. In a significant move for the company, brought about by fierce competition from smaller, cheaper cars from Japan and Europe, the design of this car was rigidly governed by what Ford engineers termed 'the limits of 2000'. In other words, the Pinto must weigh less than 2000 pounds and cost less than $2000. Sales were buoyant and Ford looked to have a winning product. Nearly 2 million Pintos were sold within 2 years of its launch.

Yet, less than 7 years later, Dr Leslie Ball – former safety chief for the NASA manned space programme and founder of the International Society of Reliability Engineers – publicly declared that 'the release to production of the Pinto was the most reprehensible decision in the history of American engineering.'[1]

So, what went wrong?

Ford Pinto: unsafe at any speed?

In May 1972, Richard Grimshaw, aged 13, was offered a lift in one of these new Ford Pintos by a friend of his family. Unfortunately, the car stalled on Interstate Route 15 and was hit from behind by another vehicle. Although this vehicle was travelling at only 35 miles an hour, the impact ruptured the Pinto's petrol tank. The escaping fumes mixed with the air in the passenger compartment, a spark ignited the mixture and the Pinto was enveloped in flames. The driver was burned to death and Grimshaw suffered 90 per cent burns and, despite a total of 52 surgical operations, the loss of his nose, one ear and four fingers.

5 years later, Grimshaw's law suit against the Ford Motor Company began. His lawyers sought punitive damages against the company by contending that Ford's decision to locate the Pinto's fuel tank only 7 inches behind the rear bumper showed a 'conscious and wilful' disregard for the safety of people who bought the car. On 11 February 1978, the jury reached its verdict and ordered Ford to pay Grimshaw $66 million in punitive damages.

The verdict was secured following the damning testimony of a senior Ford designer and the presentation in court of a confidential seven page internal company report from Ford's Environmental and Safety Engineering Division. Both these focused attention on the fact that Ford management were aware of the dangers inherent in the design and location of the Pinto's fuel tank, and yet took no action to remove or minimise these dangers.

The case against Ford

Harley F. Copp, senior design engineer with Ford for 20 years, now retired, told the Santa Anna Superior Court that the company had held numerous meetings to discuss the type of fuel tank to be used in the Pinto. Copp argued for a saddle-style tank of the kind used in the successful Capri range. This type of tank is located either side of the prop shaft and is widely regarded as the safest design possible in a small car. Copp told Ford's senior management that Ford Capris with saddle-type tanks had come through crash tests successfully. The following day, Capris with modified tanks placed, like the Pinto's, under the floor and behind the rear axle, were crash tested and leaked petrol in every case.

However, Copp testified that Ford's 'corporate management' insisted that the fuel tank be located 7 inches behind the rear bumper as this would provide a cost saving of approximately $9 dollars per car when compared with the more expensive saddle-tank design. The 'limits of 2000' could not be transgressed and the Pinto kept the rear tank design. Ford executives argued that a $9 increase could price a compact car like the Pinto out of its market, as could a marginal reduction in sales features such as the size of the boot. As one Ford engineer told the US magazine, *Mother Jones*: 'Do you realise that if we put a Capri-type tank in the Pinto you could only get one set of golf clubs in there?'[2]

Copp then told the court that the hazards presented by the design and positioning of the Pinto's fuel tank had been investigated by several independent organisations. A study in 1973 by the University of Miami's Accident Analysis Unit, examining four years of car crashes, had singled out the Pinto for comment. Under the heading 'Gas Tank Integrity/ Protection (Ford Pinto)', the Unit observed:

> In each case the gas tank was buckled and gas spewed out. In each case the interior of the vehicle was totally gutted by the ensuing fire. It is our opinion that three such conflagrations (all experienced by one rental company in a six month period) demonstrates a clear and present safety hazard to all Pinto owners.

The most damning evidence against the Ford Motor Company was the report entitled 'Fatalities associated with crash-induced fuel leakages and fires', written by the company's own Environmental and Safety Engineering Division (ESED).

By mid-1972, public concern about the safety of the Pinto prompted political action. US Congress set about drafting a set of tougher fuel tank safety standards to prevent tank explosion after an accident. Whilst these proposals were being debated, Ford senior management commissioned the confidential ESED report. On p. 5 of the report, the authors outline their analysis of the price of building fuel tank safety into Ford vehicles against the expected benefit derived from saving Ford owners from death or injury by burning.

The analysis produced the following figures:

Benefits:

Savings: 180 burn deaths, 180 serious burn injuries, 2,100 burned vehicles

Unit cost: $200,000 per death, $67,000 per injury, $700 per vehicle

Total benefit: (180 x $200,000) + (180 x $67,000) + (2,100 x $700) = $49.5 million

Costs:

Sales: 11 million cars, 1.5 million light trucks

Unit cost: $11 per car, $11 per truck.

Total cost: (11,000,000 x $11) + (1,500,000 x $11) = $137.5 million

In drawing up these figures, Ford's experts doubted the US government's statistics on fatalities from crash-induced fuel leaks and fires which estimated that between 2,000 and 3,500 such deaths occurred every year. Ford's research suggested that most of the deaths in 'fire accompanied crashes' were due to injuries caused by the initial crash impact rather than by the flames. They concluded that a figure between 600 and 700 fire deaths a year 'is probably more appropriate'.

The report pointed out that the chance of petrol spilling out from a ruptured tank was significantly greater when a car was hit from behind than from the front, side or after being rolled over. Nonetheless, Ford's engineers based their calculations of the sums at stake (if new fuel tank safety standards being proposed by Congress were adopted) on the less common hazard of 'static-rollover'. This reduced the number of burn deaths per year to 180.

Ford's calculations of the value of a human life were based on a 1972 study by the National Highway Traffic Safety Administration which sought to establish the cash cost of death in a car crash by breaking down and valuing 10 separate components, including future productivity losses, insurance administration, losses in income tax revenue, and so forth. The sum of $10,000 was established for 'victim's pain and suffering'. The overall cost to society came to $200,000. Ford also allowed $67,000 for non-fatal burn injuries.

In addition to their conservative estimate of 180 burn deaths a year, Ford safety engineers reckoned that 180 passengers a year would survive such accidents with severe burns. Adding an allowance for the cost of damaged cars, the company put the total benefit of a design change at just under $50 million. In the ESED report, this was set against the $137[.5] million costs associated with undertaking fuel tank design modifications to its cars and light trucks.

Ford safety engineers observed that the cost to the Ford Motor Company was almost three times greater than the benefits to society 'even using a number of highly favourable benefit assumptions'. The report concluded by stating that the ESED could not envisage any development which 'would make compliance with the roll-over requirement cost effective'.

No changes were made to the fuel tanks on any Ford vehicle as a result of the ESED report. It wasn't until September 1976 (in response to revised rear-impact standards imposed by the US government) that the Ford Motor Company moved the Pinto fuel tank to a safer position under the car.

Postscript

Responding to the Grimshaw case verdict, a spokesperson for Ford stated that the company would fight against 'this unreasonable and unwarranted award'. Immediately after the court hearing, the company formally appealed against the jury's decision.

Subsequently, on 7 April 1978, a Santa Ann[a] Superior Court judge ordered the $66 million punitive damages originally awarded by the jury to be reduced to $3.3 million. The judge ruled that the ratio of punitive to actual damages was excessive.

…

Notes

1. Quoted in *Sunday Times*, 12 February 1978, p. 4.

2. *Sunday Times*, 12 February 1978, p. 5.

(Source: Corbett, 1994, pp. 76–9)

Activity 5.3

Spend about **1 hour** on this activity.

Purpose: to reinforce the learning points from the case study above in relation to issues raised in this section.

Task: read Case Study 5.1 and consider the following two questions in relation to it (the hour suggested for this includes reading the case study):

1   What different controls on corporate power can you see in the case and how effective were they?

2   What does this case tell us about the third face of power (see again section 4.2 in study Session 4)?

Feedback

Two controls were apparent in the case: the first is government regulation and the second is consumer action through the legal action of Grimshaw. However, it is also important to establish why Ford didn't take any voluntary action to correct its mistakes and consider the consequences of that.

The case tells us that Ford didn't want to take any voluntary action because it was committed to the 'limits of 2000' strategy, it was concerned about sales levels, and it did not want to admit any further legal liability regarding the Pinto, and because the boot space was one of the key marketing features of the car. This is clearly shown in the advertisement. However, the effect of this was that Ford disregarded obvious safety information from internal and external sources, and to justify its strategy it employed 'unusual' approaches to accident figures which meant that the costs of changing the design were ultimately subverted by the costs of paying damages. Ford took these decisions purely on the basis of cost and strategic considerations and did not attend to any ethical or human issues in its decision making.

The third face of power refers to the way in which power is distributed throughout a society, and how different groups within a society are able to act in different ways and develop their own norms and priorities. In relation to this case, the key issue is how business and government related at the time of the events (the 1970s). Ultimately, the government, through its long-winded legislative process, was able to regulate the actions of Ford within the national boundaries of the North American market. The case also showed how the second face of power works. Internally, the senior management within Ford became so convinced of its own strategic priorities, and the internal norms within the business were so strong, that it failed to respond to any other messages or pressure that might indicate it was in the wrong. Whether this situation would arise today is a different matter, however, with the economic, legislative and political landscape of the twenty-first century being quite different from that of the internal markets of the USA in the 1970s.

We built Ford Pinto to follow in the steps of the rugged old Model T.

Back in 1911, publicity stunts were the fashion in the car business.

Like coaxing a Model T up the steps of the State Capitol in Nashville, Tenn., to impress people with its ruggedness.

But now it's sixty years later. And even though we want you to be just as impressed with Pinto's ruggedness — we figure we'd better give you some facts and figures. Not stunts.

The Pinto engine. (Above.) Rugged and reliable. Improved and perfected in more than 10 years of driving in small Ford-built cars all over the world. Easy on gas, simple to maintain.

The Pinto transmission. A floor-mounted 4-speed fully synchronized transmission is standard on Pinto. It was designed to be "lubed for life". All it should need is inspection during routine dealer maintenance.

The Pinto body. Unitized into one piece of welded steel, with steel guard rails in the door, steel reinforcements in the roof. And a surprising amount of room inside.

Extra-strength parts. Many Pinto components could be used in much bigger cars: the ball joints in the front suspension (below), the universal joint, starter motor, rear wheel bearings.

We built Ford Pinto to be a rugged, durable, basic car — a car that could follow in the footsteps of the legendary Model T.

See all the 1973 Pintos at your Ford Dealer's: 2-door sedan, 3-door Runabout, and the popular Pinto Wagon.

When you get back to basics, you get back to Ford.

Shown here is a 1973 Pinto sedan with optional whitewall tires, accent and deluxe bumper groups.

FORD PINTO
FORD DIVISION

A Ford Pinto advertisement from 1973, which emphasises the car's boot space

5.3 Conclusion

In this final study session we have attempted to extend your thinking about the different dimensions or faces of power we looked at in study Session 4, by suggesting various ways in which the power of businesses might be resisted. Government legislation (as in the case of the Ford Pinto), lobbyists and consumer groups have won several 'victories' in recent decades. The most important outcome of this has been the raising of people's awareness of how business can try to evade social responsibility in the name of profit or produ. We have consciously concluded our exploration of different ways of looking at business with a look at how you, the citizen, customer and employee could have some effect on business today.

5.4 Learning outcomes

By the end of this study session on resisting and challenging business power you should be able to:

- outline was is meant by negative business power;
- describe the main ways in which business power might be controlled.

You will have developed your learning by:

- applying your learning to a real case study: in this instance, the Ford Pinto.

Summary of Book 5

The aim of Book 5 has been to introduce you to some different ways of looking at and thinking about business. Throughout the book we have begun to criticise and break down the descriptions and accounts of the nature of business which we have hitherto taken for granted. It is safe to say that there is a 'traditional' view of business which treats business as a concrete thing (that is, reifies it), rather than as something which is emergent, and has political, social and environmental as well as economic antecedents, dimensions and effects.

There are, indeed, multiple interpretations of business. As social scientists, we can begin to examine these interpretations using the conceptual and philosophical tools of ontology and epistemology. In social science, there is frequently no right answer. It is more important to be able to reflect on what we can say about a business in terms of the resources, knowledge and perspectives we have access to. Some different interpretations of business arise because of the specific problems associated with organisations themselves: they can be analysed at different levels; there is no common understanding of 'organisational effectiveness'; when business events start and finish is often unclear; and there are different paradigms we can use to analyse business: the positivist and phenomenological being two such examples.

Business practice in the past was embedded in different contexts and could be viewed from different perspectives. Events happening in the last century can often be linked to articulations of and perspectives on business, and the emergence of particular sets of theories. It is important to realise the importance of power in this process. Power is conceived at three levels: the individual level, the organisational–cultural–structural level, and the societal–cultural–structural level. At the top two levels of analysis, power rests on the ability of certain groups to mobilise resources in their favour and establish norms and legitimacy as a result of their actions.

Globalisation is an interesting way in which to examine the operation of power at the organisational and societal levels. Globalisation has a number of drivers, and a number of advantages and disadvantages. The drivers are related to cost, markets, governments and competition, and globalisation bestows various advantages and disadvantages on the host nation and the multinational corporation. Multinationals are powerful economic actors whose actions have effects on a global scale. Globalisation has also given rise to specific industries which have a transformative effect on specific economies and their citizens (for example, India and the BPO industry, as we saw in Example 4.1).

Some business actions have been shown to cause harm to the environment, community and society. There are various ways in which corporate power can be challenged or resisted: through voluntary corporate social responsibility, governmental regulation, consumer action, or direct action by pressure groups. One thing is certain: capitalism is the dominant normative system in the Western world, and in parts of the developing world too. Any debates about corporate power in context will always be dominated by the relative power balance between government and business. Moreover, if we are to develop as critical business thinkers, it is important that we recognise that business is underpinned by power and politics, which permeate the activities of individuals, groups, organisations, economies and societies.

This is the final book of the course. We hope that B120 has provided you with a sound introduction to the issues and ideas surrounding all kinds of businesses throughout the world. Our intention, particularly in this book, has been to get you thinking. With your Study Companion you should be able to reflect not only on many aspects of the business world, but also on your own personal learning journey to this point. We wish you every success in your future study and/or working life.

The B120 team

References

Boddy, D. (2002) *Management An Introduction* (2nd edn), Harlow, Financial Times/Prentice Hall.

Bryman, A. (1989) *Research Methods and Organization Studies*, London, Sage.

Burns, T. and Stalker, G. M. (1961) *The Management of Innovation*, London, Tavistock.

Corbett, J. M. (1994) *Critical Cases in Organizational Behaviour*, Basingstoke, Macmillan.

Dahl, R. (1957) 'The concept of power', *Behavioural Science*, July, pp. 202–3.

Economist (2005) 'Busy signals: too many chiefs, not enough Indians', *The Economist*, 9 October, Vol. 376, No. 8443, p. 60.

Griffith, S. B. (1963) *Sun Tzu, The Art of War*, New York, Oxford University Press.

Klein, N.(2001) *No Logo*, London, Flamingo.

Maslow, A. (1943) 'A theory of human motivation', *Psychological Review* , Vol. 50, No. 4, pp. 370–96.

Maslow, A. (1970) *Motivation and Personality* (2nd edn), New York, Harper & Row.

Morgan, G. (1986) *Images of Organization,* Thousand Oaks, CA/London, Sage.

Nayyar, D. (2002) 'Themes in trade and industrialization' in Suneja, V. (ed.) *Policy Issues for Business*, London, Sage/The Open University, pp. 191–209.

Porter, M. E. (1990) 'How competitive forces shape strategy', *Harvard Business Review*, Vol. 57, No. 2, March–April, pp. 137–45.

Sloman, J. and Sutcliffe, M. (2000) 'Multinational corporations' in Suneja, V. (ed.) *Understanding Business: Markets*, London, Routledge/Milton Keynes, The Open University, pp. 196–212.

Townley, B.(1994) *Reframing HRM: Power, Ethics and the Subject of Work*, London, Sage.

Vroom, V. H. (1964) *Work and Motivation*, New York, John Wiley.

Waddock, S. A. and Graves, S. B. (1997) 'The corporate social performance – financial performance link', *Strategic Management Journal*, Vol. 18, No. 4, pp. 303–19.

Watson, T. (2002) *Organising and Managing Work: Organisational, Managerial and Strategic Behaviour in Theory and Practice*, Harlow, Financial Times/ Prentice Hall.

Weber, M. (1964) *The Theory of Social and Economic Organization* (trans. A. M. Henderson and T. Parsons; ed. with introduction by T. Parsons), London, Collier Macmillan.

Wyss, J. (2005) 'eBay's popularity spurs growth of dropoff stores', *Miami Herald*, 22 August [online] http://www.quikdrop.com/press/08.23.05-miamiherald.pdf (accessed 6 March 2006).

Acknowledgements

Grateful acknowledgement is made to the following sources for permission to reproduce material in this book:

Text

Case Studies 1.1 and 5.1: Corbett, J. M. (1994) *Critical Cases in Organisational Behaviour*, The Macmillan Press Ltd, reproduced with permission of Palgrave Macmillan; *Case Study 4.1:* Watson, T. (2002) *Organising and Managing Work*, Pearson Education Limited. © Pearson Education Limited 2002; *Example 4.1: The Economist*, 'Busy signals: too many chiefs, not enough Indians', *The Economist* , 9 October 2005, Vol. 376, Issue 8443 © The Economist Newspaper Limited.

Photographs/Illustrations

Page 5 taken from: http://www.talsico.com/newsletters/Newsletter2Article2. htm; *Page 11:* © Ted Goff; *Pages 21 and 29:* © Randy Glasbergen; *Page 24:* © Mary Evans Picture Library; *Page 26:* © Rex Features; *Page 28:* reproduced with permission from McDonald's Restaurants Limited; *Page 37:* © Helene Rogers/Alamy; *Page 52:* © INSADCO Photography/Alamy; *Page 57:* © The Advertising Archives.

Cover

Front cover image: © Photodisc.

Module team

B120 team

Dr Anja Schaefer
Dr Nik Winchester
Dr Warren Smith
Dr Vira Krakhmal
Barry Jones, *Curriculum Manager*
Carey Stephens
Susan Hughes
Rosie McGookin
Val O'Connor, *Curriculum Assistant*

The original course team

Dr Diane Preston, *Course Team Chair*
Patricia McCarthy, *Course Manager*
Dr Kirstie Ball
Penny Marrington
Fran Myers
Dr Anja Schaefer
Dr George Watson
Rita Gregory, *Course Team Assistant*
Val O'Connor, *Course Team Assistant*

Other contributors

Professor Judy Day
Dr Lorna J. Eller
Mick Fryer
Jonathan Winship

External examiner

Kate Greenan, *Professor of Management Education and Head of School of Accounting, Ulster University*

Developmental testers

Linda Fisher
Adam Messer
John Messer
Marina Ramtohul

Critical readers

Patricia Coffey, *Senior Lecturer, University of Brighton Business School*
Clare Cromarty, *OUBS Associate Lecturer*
Patricia Dawson, *Principal Lecturer, Thames Valley University, retired*

Helen Higson, *Director of Undergraduate Studies, Aston Business School*
Beverly Leeds, *Principal Lecturer, University of Central Lancashire*
Nigel Walton, *OUBS Associate Lecturer*

Production team

Martin Brazier, *Graphic Designer*
Angela Davies, *Media Assistant*
Richard Dobson, *Editor*
Hannah Eiseman-Renyard, *Editor*
Diane Hopwood, *Rights Assistant*
Lee Johnson, *Media Project Manager*
Siggy Martin, *Assistant Print Buyer*
Katy Nyaaba, *Media Assistant*
Jill Somerscales, *Editor*

The original production team

Holly Clements, *Media Assistant*
Lene Connolly, *Print Buyer*
Jonathan Davies, *Graphic Designer*
Julie Fletcher, *Media Project Manager*
Fiona Harris, *Editor*
Diane Hopwood, *Compositor*
Kate Hunter, *Editor*
Jon Owen, *Graphic Artis*t
Deana Plummer, *Picture Researcher*
Nikki Smith, *Assistant Print Buyer*
Jill Somerscales, *Editor*

B120 An Introduction to Business Studies

Book 1   What is a business?

Book 2   An introduction to human
resource management in business

Book 3   An introduction to accounting and
finance in business

Book 4   An introduction to marketing
in business

Book 5   Different ways of looking at business

The Open University Business School holds triple
AACSB, EQUIS and AMBA accreditation

www.open.ac.uk/business-school

The Open University

ISBN 978-1-8487-3589-7

9 781848 735897

ARCHAEOLOGICAL MONOGRAPH SERIES: 8

Clogh Oughter Castle, Co. Cavan: Archaeology, History and Architecture

Conleth Manning